How About That!

Jimmy Crum: Fifty Years of Cliffhangers and Barn-Burners

Jimmy Crum and Carole Gerber

FINE LINE GRAPHICS

COLUMBUS, OHIO

For permission for reprints or excerpts, contact Carole Gerber, 1357 W. Lane Avenue, Columbus, OH 43221. Phone: 614/486-6711.

International Standard Book Number 0-9638284-0-1

Cover design: Jane Fuller
Cover photo: Joyce E. Brown
*   Petty Studio*

Contents

Dedicated to the women in my life

Kelly, Michalea, Miriam

Acknowledgments

In fifty years of broadcasting, I've met and worked with some of the most creative, knowledgeable, and hard-working people in the world. If I began naming names, as I would like to, the list would fill another book. I can only hope that you know who you are, and understand how much your friendship and support have meant to me.

Those same sentiments hold true for the children I've been privileged to meet through my association with Recreation Unlimited, Children's Hospital, Easter Seals, Special Olympics, the Heinzerling Memorial Foundation, and other organizations. These children have been as important to me as my own children and grandchildren, and I have boundless respect for the parents, doctors, nurses, therapists, and administrators who care for them.

I also deeply appreciate the generosity and thoughtfulness of my associates in the press, radio and television who have helped me with any and all causes having to do with children.

This acknowledgment would not be complete without thanking the athletes, coaches, trainers, managers and others who have allowed me, as a reporter, to be part of their lives. Your friendships have helped to make the past fifty years the most enjoyable a man could have.

Finally, I must name three names. Special thanks go to my co-author, Carole Gerber, whose persistence, patience and humor have kept this book on track, and to Bob Greene, whose foreword provides a heartfelt introduction to it.

I also want to thank Vlade Janakievski, owner of Easy Living, who refused to accept payment for all the sandwiches, bagel sticks and chocolate chip cookies Carole and I ate as we slaved over the final pages.

Jimmy Crum

Preface

This book exists because somebody twisted my arm. Several years ago, I spoke to a journalism class at Ohio State University taught by a free-lance writer named Carole Gerber. I shared anecdotes about my experiences as a sports reporter with her students and answered their questions about the field of broadcasting. After class, Carole said, "Jim, you are so enthusiastic about what you do. Why don't you think about writing a book?"

I told her the thought of writing a book had never crossed my mind, and that was the end of it—until the next quarter, when I was again a guest speaker in her newswriting class. After class, Carole once again asked whether I had given any thought to writing a book. This time, she offered to help me do it.

She suggested, to get us started, that I keep a tape recorder and a pencil and pad in my car for the next six months. She urged me to dictate or write down any thoughts or memories about my career, my lifelong interest in sports, and my first-hand experiences with Woody Hayes, Fred Taylor, Bobby Knight and other sports figures. I thought it might be fun to record my memories, even if nothing ever came of it, and I decided to take Carole's advice.

After about three months of recording my thoughts, I began to believe my experiences and recollections might be the basis for a book. At that point, Carole and I got together and discussed how we would work as collaborators. After six months, I had so doggone many notes that I thought, "Gee, we might be able to write half a dozen books."

In 1986, Carole and I started out on a venture we thought would take 18 months to two years. Seven years, a few different OSU coaches, and a dozen of my sports commentaries later, we have finally finished it.

Thanks, Carole, for twisting my arm. It really didn't hurt too much.

Jimmy Crum

Foreword

Jimmy Crum is the most famous person in the history of broadcasting in central Ohio, but he would be the first to tell you that becoming famous is a relatively easy thing.

It can happen in a day; a headline can propel a man or a woman into the public's consciousness. Jimmy became famous the hard way, through professionalism and long years of excellence in his job, yet the fact that every person who has lived in the Columbus area since the invention of television knows his name—that fact, Jimmy would tell you, is not his legacy.

He knew Woody Hayes well, and Jack Nicklaus, and Archie Griffin and Jerry Lucas and John Havlicek and every other luminary who made his or her name on Ohio fields of play. John Glenn watched Jimmy Crum on Channel 4 at night, and Jim Rhodes watched him, and John Galbreath and Dave Thomas and every other leader of government and business. The prominent names in Jimmy's life are impressive, but they aren't what matters.

What matters is the kind of person he is. It would have been very easy for Jimmy to coast through life on his celebrity—when your face and name are known to 100 percent of a metropolitan area's population, you can get away, if you so desire, with just wandering around accepting hellos and accolades. Jimmy could have gone through life dining out on his smile, telling sports anecdotes to strangers and basking in the false glow of fame.

He didn't do it. What he did—most often in the quietest of ways—was go out of his way to help forgotten children, virtually every day of his life. Between broadcasts he would get in his car and go to visit children without sight, children without hearing, children born with grievous disabilities. He did it through formal organizations, yes, but just as often he did it on his own. He would hear about a child who needed encouragement, and he would get in his car and he would go visit.

Not once for a certain child in need; not twice or three times. The children Jimmy cared for needed a friend, and Jimmy became their friend for life. Many of them are adults now, and they still know Jimmy, he still keeps in touch, and their lives are better because Jimmy has been a part of them.

The public really doesn't know about all of this. Central Ohio has embraced Jimmy because of the superlative and honest job he has done on the air all these years. In this book you will read about his career in broadcasting—and it has been a career of great success. So much of Jimmy is so familiar to his viewers—from the look on his face to the sound of his voice to those plaid sports coats—that most viewers long ago began to take his presence for granted. They'll miss it now that he is retiring, and when they think about it they will be mightily impressed by the craftsmanship he has brought to his work—the authority of his presentation, the flawlessness of his on-air delivery, the familiarity with the subjects he is covering.

But, again, Jimmy would tell you that this is the least of it.

I have known Jimmy for more than 30 years. The first job I ever had in the news business was sitting beside him in St. John Arena, keeping statistics for him during the Lucas-Havlicek era of Ohio State basketball. As a kid back then I was his fan, and now that I am his friend I am still his fan. He is wonderful at what he does.

Jimmy's true legacy, though, is the warmth he has shown to those children, whose eyes would light up every time he came to see them again. Some of them, of course, could not see him, but they would hear this voice as he arrived, and they would light up all the same. He spoke to millions upon millions of central Ohio sports fans over the years on television, but what he said, one-on-one, to those children who counted on him was every bit as important as anything he said into a microphone.

His story is in this book; now that Jimmy is leaving the air, we can all keep this volume as a reminder of his days in Columbus, and ours. I mentioned that he is the most famous person in the history of central Ohio broadcasting; he will probably keep that title forever, because with the fragmentation of modern media it is not likely that anyone in the future will ever come along who will have the impact that Jimmy did.

Fame is fleeting, though; fame floats off into the night sky. Jimmy will be remembered for many things, but he has achieved something better than fame, something that few public men and women can claim to have earned. It is this:

He is loved.

Bob Greene

1

♦

From Radio to Sports and Back Again

My broadcast career began on a high note fifty-three years ago in Mansfield, Ohio, where I made my debut at age twelve as a boy soprano on WMAN Radio's Saturday morning talent show. I usually teamed up for these unpaid warblings with Avis LaVerne Forrest, a girl alto from nearby Galion. Together we treated listeners to such children's classics as "Little Sir Echo" and "Blue Skies."

The hour-long Saturday morning show was so popular, probably because of all the friends and relatives who tuned in, that in 1942 Avis LaVerne and I were asked by the station to do a fifteen-minute evening show on Thursdays. The weeknight show was sponsored by Faust the Jeweler and provided listeners with more children's classics.

Our only compensation for these appearances was a small measure of local fame—heady stuff for kids whose friends' careers began and ended with singing in their school choirs. Avis LaVerne and I enthusiastically continued our weekly duets for another two years until puberty struck, rendering me an alto overnight. Soon afterwards the alto dropped to bass.

Because I could no longer hit the high notes, I put my singing career on hold, set common sense aside and plunged briefly—very briefly—into playing football. My decision to go out for the school team was a foolish one. At fourteen, I had reached my full height of 5'8" and weighed only 128 lbs. My reasoning was that although I was small, I was a fighter. I'd been born prematurely and spent the first sixteen weeks of my life in an orange crate incubator struggling to catch up. Clearly, I was a survivor.

This desire to survive didn't help much when it came to football, though. I was too short for football, too skinny for football and, in 1944, too dumb to know any better. However, I was quickly educated about my shortcomings before the season even officially began. In August I was injured in a scrimmage by bigger players on my own team and wound up in the hospital with my collarbone broken in three places.

Although I didn't realize it at the time, my first and only football injury was a turning point in my life. It drove home, forcefully and all too painfully, the realization that, unlike my taller, huskier classmates at Mansfield Senior High, I was probably never going to be a quarterback, an outfielder, or a forward.

Because a deep interest in sports was something I shared with my father, this disappointment was much harder to take than having puberty wreck my singing career, which I hadn't taken too seriously anyway. Like many fathers of his era, Dad was a forceful and opinionated man who felt his authority within the family should go unquestioned. I was a natural questioner, especially during adolescence, and our mutual love of sports was a spot of tranquility in an often stormy relationship.

From the time I was a small boy in the 1930's, Dad—who held a sedentary job as a Westinghouse executive—would take me up to Cleveland with him to watch the Indians when they played at League Park. My childhood heroes were all ball players, and even today the names Hal Trosky, Jeff Heath, Ray Mack and Roy "Thunder" Weatherly make my heart beat a little faster. It was tough to admit to myself that I didn't have the athletic ability to follow in their footsteps—or even to keep my collarbone out of harm's way during a football scrimmage.

But I'm a born optimist, so I didn't stay down in the dumps too long. If I couldn't play sports, well, I could certainly talk about them, and luck soon intervened to help me get started. When the sports director at

Mansfield's WMAN left to go to WAKR in Akron, the station manager, who knew me from my "Little Sir Echo" days, called and asked me to audition for the job. True, I was only fourteen, but the beauty of radio is that my age didn't matter. What was important was how I sounded—thanks to puberty, much older—and what I knew about sports—thanks to my dad, quite a bit.

So, on Christmas Eve 1942, I began my first paid job in broadcasting as a sportscaster and disc jockey. I held the job for three years, working fulltime during the summer and part-time while school was in session. I enjoyed the job thoroughly, especially the personal creativity the station manager allowed me. I was probably the only guy in the country who regularly played Nat King Cole's "The Christmas Song" in the middle of the summer—you could take bets on it.

For a 40-hour week, I was paid fifteen dollars. I earned an extra dollar each week by vacuuming studios A and B and the station's long center hallway. At last, my as-yet unrecognized physical abilities were being rewarded! In fact, on an hourly basis, vacuuming paid more than broadcasting, but I was never tempted to go into cleaning fulltime.

Working at WMAN consumed nearly all my free time until I graduated from high school in 1946. In fact, I was so busy that I didn't have a single date until the senior prom, when I got up from my microphone and decided I needed at least one social event to recall nostalgically in later years. One of my closest high school friends, Chug Floro, obliged by fixing me up with a classmate, Esther Bishop, and arranging a double date.

Esther and I hit it off pretty well at the prom, but on the way to the after-prom festivities we both fell asleep in Chug's backseat and things didn't get much livelier. The highlight of the evening occurred when we woke up briefly to say goodnight at her house several hours later. Even though we slept together on our first date, apparently Esther felt that special spark was missing and we never went out again.

Along with many of my classmates, I was busy trying to figure out serious stuff like what to do after graduation, so my failure in the romance department didn't seem too important. Although World War II was over when I graduated from Mansfield High in June, 1946, young men were still being drafted and I expected to receive the call. I wanted to be in the Marine Corps, so I enlisted right after graduation and—hoping to put my broadcast experience to work—applied for Special Services.

My request was granted and, after a brief stay at Cherry Point, North Carolina, where I wrote for the Marine newspaper, *The Windsock*, I spent the remainder of my hitch doing play-by-play broadcasts of intra-service baseball, basketball and football games for Armed Forces Radio. Although I did a little traveling overseas, most of my time between 1946 and 1948 was spent broadcasting at Marine bases on the east coast.

Covering sports was exactly what I wanted to do, and my time in the Marines was a wonderful experience. Before enlisting I'd hardly been out of Ohio, so the opportunity to travel was exciting. So was the fact that I got to spend two years being paid to learn my trade. Even better was finding out that the GI Bill would pay for my college education when my hitch was up—something I hadn't realized when I enlisted.

Deciding where to go to college was easy. My sergeant in the Marines had gone to Ohio University and when he showed me his yearbook, I fell in love with the pastoral beauty of the campus and decided to enroll. When I got to Athens in the fall of 1948, however, this picture postcard quality had been temporarily thrown out of focus by hordes of former GIs needing housing. Like other campuses, OU responded quickly to this demand by throwing up barracks and Quonset huts.

The temporary housing is long gone now and the area, known as the East Green, is one of the prettiest places on campus. In my day, though, it was unofficially referred to as "Hog Island"—probably because pigs like to wallow in mud. Regular flooding of the Hocking River created knee-deep piles of the stuff before the Army Corps of Engineers rechanneled the Hocking River some years later. Whenever it flooded during my college years, planks were thrown down over the mess. And heaven help the Hog Islander who'd had one too many on a Saturday night and lost his balance on the way home!

Walking the plank didn't put a damper on my enthusiasm for college, though. Then, as now, OU's journalism school had a fine reputation and I tried to take full advantage of the opportunities it offered me. Because there was no TV journalism curriculum in 1948—television was in its earliest infancy and no one expected anything so foolish to last—I majored in radio under the watchful guidance of Professor Vincent Jukes.

Vinnie, who then headed OU's Radio School, took great interest in his students. If he saw any glimmer of talent, he'd take you under his wing. I was one of a number of fledgling broadcast journalists who benefited from his guidance and support. I owe a lot to Vinnie, both for his faith in my abilities and for what he taught me about broadcasting.

It was quite obvious that Vinnie's faith in my future was a lot stronger than my father's. Although he thought my high school experience at WMAN was okay—it had, after all, kept me out of trouble with girls—Dad probably hoped I'd get rid of the broadcasting bug while I was in the service. It wasn't that he didn't think I had talent; he simply believed broadcasting was a poor way for a grown man to make a living. No doubt his concern was justified.

Listening to radio was a popular pastime, but there wasn't much money to be made from broadcasting. Television was for the few who could afford sets. And watching and talking about sports, in Dad's opinion, was what adults did for recreation—not how they supported families.

He took a dim view of my part-time radio jobs during my freshman year at OU, and put his foot down in 1949 when I told him I planned to accept a summer job at WMAN Radio in Mansfield. Since I hadn't yet turned twenty-one and because I was living in his home, I reluctantly agreed to take the factory job he'd arranged for me with his company.

Working as a laborer at Westinghouse paid much more than I'd have made at the station, but the money wasn't important to me. It should have been. With help from the GI Bill, I was paying my own way through college. But back when I'd fallen in love with broadcasting at age fourteen, my foggy plans for the future had been unsullied by financial concerns. Years later, much to Dad's disappointment, I was still choosing love over money.

It wasn't until 1953, when I started with what is now Channel 4 Television, that my career choice finally received his approval. Or maybe he just decided to accept the fact that I was never going to come to my senses!

Except for the summer job at Westinghouse, all my school vacations during high school and college were spent at WMAN in Mansfield. I worked with some wonderful people there who helped me gain experience in everything from the mundane to the magnificent. Earl Black, Ski Fields, Bob Horn and Lillian Boock were my friends as well as my co-workers. So were Bessie Blackman, Dick Oram, Bob Christopher, Ocie Chandler, Mark Lucas and Jim Minium.

It was because these folks treated me like a colleague instead of like a kid that so many great opportunities came my way at WMAN. One of my first jobs for the station was teaming up with Jim Minium for live "Man on the Street" interviews sponsored by King's Shoe Store. Jim and I would switch back and forth, with one of us chatting up an interviewee while the other collared the next person. Of course, the broadcasts were peppered with thanks to our sponsor.

I'll never forget the time I interviewed a woman who said she'd come into town to buy shoes for her kids, who were trailing along behind. Since the program was sponsored by King's Shoes, I immediately went for the obvious and began plugging the quality of the store's merchandise on the air.

"Huh!" she snorted. "I wouldn't go into that damn place if you paid me!" That was not the kind of free advertising King's was looking for, and from that day forward the store declined to sponsor further programs for WMAN.

Fortunately, the station didn't blame me for such mishaps. In the spring of 1946, when I was a senior in high school, I got to report on Mansfield's biggest social event in years. Harold Robinson and I covered the wedding of Humphrey Bogart and Lauren Bacall at Malabar Farm, the home of Mansfield's favorite son and only famous author, Louis Bromfield.

Mr. Bromfield later invited me, along with other OU students, to Malabar to Phi Delta Theta rush parties. I was thrilled to be at Bromfield's parties, and I joined his fraternity. But the rush parties were not nearly as exciting for me as reporting first-hand on the wedding of Bogie and Bacall.

Recently, I had the honor of once again seeing Lauren Bacall. Last January I was in Beverly Hills for the National Easter Seal Telethon meetings, and had gone to Trader Vic's for dinner. Shortly after my companions and I were seated, Miss Bacall and a lady friend sat down at a nearby table.

I waited until they had ordered their drinks, then went over, introduced myself, and told her that as a 17-year-old reporter for WMAN in

Mansfield, I had covered her wedding to Bogie. When I mentioned the name of Judge Herb Shettler, the man who'd married them, she realized I was on the level and invited me to sit down. We chatted for a few minutes and I found her to be a very gracious lady. What a thrill it was to share those memories together!

Lauren Bacall's wedding was definitely the most beautiful event I covered as a radio reporter, but there were also other thrilling events. In 1948 I had the honor of introducing President Harry Truman to a nation-wide audience when he made a train stop in nearby Crestline, Ohio. That same year I spent ninety-six sleepless but exciting hours covering the whereabouts of murderers John Coulter West and Robert Murl Daniels.

The two escapees had killed the farm superintendent at the Mansfield Reformatory, along with his wife and child, before continuing on a murder spree that left four more dead and most people terrified. No one felt safe for a few days until Daniels was shot by police at a roadblock near Van Wert, Ohio. West was apprehended and later executed.

Meanwhile, during the academic years 1948 to 1952, I continued plugging away at my college courses while working at a couple of radio jobs on the side. In addition to working for free at OU's station, WOUI, I also worked for nearly nothing at Athens' WATH Radio during my freshman and sophomore years.

Every afternoon found me out in front of Butler Brothers' store doing my "Man on the Street" interviews. Sponsored, of course, by Butler Brothers, my job entailed collaring people as they walked by, asking why they were in town, and plugging Butler's merchandise as a "must-see" during their visits.

The bait used to lure them within my grasp was a small television set in Butler's window showing "Ruth Lyons' 50/50 Club" being broadcast live from Cincinnati. Since TV was still a novelty, passers-by would stop and gape at the soundless picture for several minutes, giving me plenty of time to chat them up and make my pitch.

A bashful person would probably have found this job nerve-wracking, but being at a loss for words has never been among my shortcomings. Those old "Man on the Street" shows gave me fine experience in sizing people up and handling the inevitable boo-boos that are bound crop up during live broadcasts. And if I happened to misjudge my victim and pounce on an excessively dull interviewee, I quickly learned to swing the conversation back to Butler's fabulous deals.

Sometimes the interviews were anything but dull, and those people presented a different set of problems. One afternoon while plugging away for Butler Brothers I happened to stop a young woman who said she'd come in from the country to find out the results of a test. Since she didn't look or talk like an OU student, I thought she might have an interesting story for the radio audience.

As it turned out, "interesting" was an understatement. She was in Athens, she said, to find out the results of the blood test required to take out a marriage certificate and, what's more, she'd "done gone and failed it." Needless to say, I jumped right in with a word about the sponsor!

This ability to control the conversation is critical in broadcast journalism because interviews almost always must be shoehorned into very short time slots. The importance of knowing how to cut someone off politely is a skill that most new broadcast journalists struggle with, but it's one I learned at an early age—thanks to my experience interviewing men and women on the street.

Leaving Butler Brothers behind, in March, 1950 I accepted an offer from WRFD Radio in Worthington to cover the state high school basketball tournaments. In 1951 I began covering Ohio State football games for the WRFD folks. The exposure and experience I got covering those events was great, but traveling to cover games and tournaments wreaked havoc on my class schedule.

Because so many former GIs held jobs while attending school, most professors were understanding when students occasionally missed a class. Several times, though, I had to be gone for a whole week and, rather than take a low mark, I'd drop the course in which I'd fallen hopelessly behind.

Like many students today, I didn't keep very good track of my accumulating college credits. No one was more surprised than I when I turned up thirteen credits short after four years at OU. At the time, I had to make a practical choice between school and work in a life crowded with many obligations. I left without taking my degree and carried that disappointment with me for years.

My disappointment turned to joy in 1989 when—in a surprise move that left me flabbergasted—Ohio University President Charles Ping awarded me my diploma as part of a ceremony for distinguished alumni. Although not officially an alum, I had received other awards from OU, so I was expecting another honorary certificate. I wasn't prepared for was the tremendous excitement I felt when I received that diploma. Becoming a father, a grandfather, meeting President Reagan, receiving awards—I've been part of many moving and exciting occasions. But none matched the emotion I felt when I became an official alumnus of Ohio University.

I remember those action-packed days at OU fondly. Besides going to school and working, I had followed Louis Bromfield's advice and pledged Phi Delta Theta. To show our respect, new pledges were required to recite a ridiculous spiel to frat members each time we entered the house. At the time, I could never get the spiel right—and as punishment spent a lot of time kissing the blarney stone in front of the frat house. Today I can recall every golden word.

"I, ye most honored masters of the sacred sanctorium of virtues, morals and righteousness, condescend to the lowest human level and listen to the pleas of this impious imp, this nefarious neophyte, this poor, piteous, palpitating pledge, James W. Crum, who seeks to be granted the most wondrous privilege of passing through these ponderous portals. Piteous woefully weak though I may be, I promise without reservation to consecrate my every act while within this palatial palace to the will of my most beloved and respected masters."

In addition to the time required to kiss the blarney stone and keep up with other important fraternity activities, I was also busy trying to keep a sorority girl from Chagrin Falls from dropping me because of my extended work-related absences during weekend social events. Talk about scheduling problems!

Shortly after my girlfriend returned my frat pin with the words, "You care more about that damned radio station than you do me!" I received a call from an OU alumna in Columbus telling me about a television job at WLWC, Channel 3—now Channel 4. I talked station manager Jimmy Leonard into hiring me as sports director in 1952, only three years after the station went on the air on April 3, 1949.

During those three years, WLWC had already done some exciting things. It had broadcast the first remote of a Columbus Redbird baseball game the same month it went on the air. Another first occurred on

September 24, 1949, when the station was the first to air an Ohio State University football game. In June of the following year, WLWC was the first to broadcast Ohio State's graduation ceremonies.

From what I'd seen and heard, it was clear the station was going places, and I wanted to go with it and help it grow. Selling the station manager on my experience wasn't hard—my record spoke for itself—but convincing him I had the face for the job was another matter.

Mr. Leonard was a fine man and an honest one. Whenever I've been tempted to get a swelled head, I think of a remark he made when he hired me. "Jimmy, television is a visual medium and you must realize by now that you're no Adonis," he said, referring to the handsome Greek who'd dazzled Aphrodite, the goddess of love and beauty.

I didn't think I was that bad, but he had a point—especially when it came to my ears. My right one sticks out more than the left. This was especially apparent when I was younger and thinner. Jimmy Leonard couldn't make me look like a Greek god for my television debut but he could and did do something about that ear—which was definitely a "sticking point" with him.

He insisted I flatten it against my head with a wad of chewing gum during my first couple of years on the air. If I'd come to the job encumbered with even a shred of false vanity, Mr. Leonard did away with it.

He's not the only one who's ever kidded me about my looks. Here's what my friend, former *Citizen-Journal* sportswriter Kaye Kessler, said about me in 1983 at a roast to honor my 30 years of broadcasting and community service work:

"When he was young and had hair, very dark, just like Howard Cosell and everybody else once had, Jimmy also had a body like a pool cue and the appearance of a man being choked until his eyeballs bulged. Happily, Jimmy's body finally has grown into his eyes, but his head has never grown too large for the many hats he could wear—if he wore hats."

Kaye's comments were all in fun and no one laughed harder than I did. But what he said about managing not to get a swelled head is absolutely right. I've long since unstuck my ear and lost my pool cue shape with, as far as I know, no complaints from viewers. But I have been consistent about one thing—keeping my ego under control.

It's also been easy for me to be a good sport about the comments I get about my wild sports coats and pants. They've become my trademark, and I enjoy the ribbing I take for my "distinctive" way of dressing.

I have always enjoyed wearing bright colors, but when I first came to Channel 4 in 1953, I wanted to make a serious impression so I wore the types of dark suits and ties worn by everyone else at the station. Little by little, though, I got back into wearing the bright sports coats I preferred. People began to talk about them, and I began to get wild sports coats as gifts.

About a third of the dozens of sports coats I own once belonged to a dear friend, the late Charlie Hill of Scioto Downs fame. Charlie had closets full of crazy sports coats, and he once told me after I kidded him about one of them, "There'll be a day after I pass on that you'll have some of these coats for yourself."

I never thought about it until after his funeral in 1990. Jim Rhodes and I were pallbearers, and when Charlie's wife, LaVerne, talked with us at the service, she told me that when she was feeling up to it, she'd have me over to get some of Charlie's coats. She has kept her word, and every six months or so, LaVerne will give me some more of his sports coats. Because of my long friendship with Charlie Hill, those coats are really special to me.

Another special sports coat is one I got from the late Waldo Walker, my veterinarian. Walt was a size 48 or 50, so I had to have the coat cut down. It's the only wintertime coat I've got that looks as wild as my summertime coats—it's a wool patchwork quilt design. I wear it on dreary days and it never fails to elicit comments.

I'll never forget a comment about my clothes I overheard a few years ago when my wife, Miriam, and I were at OU attending a homecoming event. Homecoming that year coincided with Halloween, which has become a major "happening" in Athens, Ohio. College students from all over the midwest gather for two days of wild partying. The town just goes crazy.

Miriam and I were standing on Court Street with former OU baseball coach Bob Wren, a Phi Delta Theta fraternity brother, and his wife, Lois. As usual, I had on a wild sports jacket. The four of us were enjoying watching the human parade, when we noticed three guys dressed like prison convicts walking our way.

They'd gone whole hog with striped clothes and faces painted to look like they'd been beaten up. They even had their wrists chained together. As they came weaving down the street, it was obvious that—like many in the crowd—they were about three sheets to the wind.

When they got within a few feet of us, though, one of them suddenly seemed to sober up. He stopped in his tracks, pointed at me, and shouted at the top of his lungs: "Jesus Christ! There's somebody dressed up like Jimmy Crum!"

That was the only time in my career I've been accused of impersonating myself. No one laughed harder than I did.

2

◆

*My Early Years
in Television*

When I first began working at WCMH, I was speaking
literally when I said I'd go to the mat for my job. Wrestling was my
first—and for a while—my only beat when I was hired as sports director,
primarily because back then few local stations had the equipment or the
manpower to cover major sports.

And since our newscasts at six and eleven mainly consisted of showing "Three-City Final" with Peter Grant out of Cincinnati, my news
reporting duties were limited to a few minutes of telling viewers what I'd
gleaned from the wire services. It was definitely a case of what journalists call "rip and read" reporting.

That doesn't mean I wasn't busy, though. During my first few years
at the station I worked seven days a week. Since everything was live,
much of my time was spent announcing programs and identifying the station's call letters each time we signed on and off the air. Because air time
was cheap and because I had learned to use all the equipment, I also was
able to write, shoot, produce and direct a number of half-hour shows.

These opportunities to be creative almost made up for having to cover wrestling. Not that it wasn't fun, but there are only so many ways to describe a hammerlock. I'd gotten experience reporting on wrestling matches when I worked in radio and had to paint word pictures of events that viewers couldn't see. Providing television commentary was easier because viewers were able to see the shenanigans I was describing.

The difference was that I knew the matches were rigged, but the viewers at home and in our studio audience apparently took them seriously. Every Saturday afternoon for two hours, 125 screaming fans would crowd into the studio to watch the free matches. The room had no air conditioning and no windows, and the onlookers were soon as sweaty as the wrestlers.

No one involved with the program was more polished than Al Haft, who promoted the matches. Al put out a program for each match titled Haft Nelson, a pun on the wrestling hold "half-Nelson." For fifteen cents, fans could read about contestants, fan clubs and other wrestling news. On the inside cover of each issue was a "lucky number." Those fans lucky enough to have their numbers drawn won prizes ranging from a free lunch at Johnny's & Ray's Food Bar to a dozen free pictures of wrestlers.

On the literary side, Haft Nelson featured such stirring writing as this description of one of the wrestlers: "What manner of man is this who breathes the fire of a dragon and possesses the strength of a bull elephant?" The fans ate it up.

Al, a former wrestler, teamed with a partner and began promoting matches throughout the midwest shortly after World War I. By the early 1950's, matches began to be televised and Haft's became the name in wrestling. At his zenith, he packed as many as five thousand fans into the bleachers of Haft's Acre, his rickety old arena at the corner of Goodale and Park. I got to know Al well because I did some of his publicity and, besides covering the matches held at Channel 4's studio, was also the ring announcer for many of his other matches.

Al also worked with a man named Clarence Nonemaker, who was his matchmaker. Early on, Clarence and Al let me in on what was really happening so I could use my commentary to the best advantage. A more practical reason for telling me things were rigged was that all the matches had to be over by the time I signed the program off the air. Since the entire spectacle was a fake, this never created a problem. When it was time to end, Clarence would signal the wrestlers by lighting a cigarette. Within thirty seconds one of them would pin the other, and the match would be over.

Occasionally, I was asked to be part of the action. Once when I was doing the ring announcing for a match at a county fair in Pomeroy, Ohio, I was set up to have a pair of fake glasses knocked off by the wrestler who was supposed to lose the match. The ring had been set up hastily on ground that wasn't level, and the slight tilt in the ring threw everyone off balance.

When it came time for the "attack," both the wrestler and I lost our balance. As we stumbled, his arm dropped and he accidentally walloped me a good one across the throat. His apology lasted all the way back to Columbus.

The idea of sports events being rigged sounds shocking, but professional wrestling has always had the reputation of being long on showmanship and short on genuine competition. That's why no one at the station batted an eye at providing the arena and the coverage for these weekly spectacles. WCMH didn't charge for the tickets and, aside from getting advertisers to pay for the air time, didn't profit from the matches.

The fans certainly did, though, at least in terms of whiling away Saturday afternoons screaming their lungs out over the likes of Buddy "Nature Boy" Rogers, Ray "Thunder" Stern, "Irish Mike" Clancy and "The Great Scott," a 233-pounder from Scotland. Other favorites included "Leaping Tiger" Vansky, and "Mysterious" Durango, who always wore a stocking mask. They were all my friends—nice guys and good athletes who knew how to put on a show for the rabid fans who turned out to watch them in that sweatbox of a studio.

Some of the fiercest fans were gentle-looking old ladies—one of whom once bopped local wrestler Frank Talaber with her purse after a match. Inside this elderly woman's handbag was a brick that inflicted a wound on Talaber's head that required medical treatment.

The only time I've ever had my number removed from the phone directory was between 1954 and 1957 when I covered wrestling. Until I got an unlisted number, it wasn't uncommon for my wife, Miriam, and me to be awakened at two or three o'clock in the morning by a call from an angry fan chewing me out about a match. On the other hand, these people could also be very kind. When Miriam and I were married in 1954, wrestling fans showered us with hand-crocheted doilies and knickknacks.

Although wrestling drew one of the largest and fiercest studio audiences, our other live shows in the early 1950's also fared well. Evening viewers were treated to a country-western show called "Meetin' Time at Moore's," hosted by Sally Flowers, Billy Scott and Charlie Cessner. A popular morning show, this one hosted by Spook Beckman, was "Shoot the Works," which relied heavily on audience participation.

The live set provided a perfect arena for Spook to crack up audiences with his antics. Every St. Patrick's Day, for example, he'd dye his hair green. The live audience loved it, but the folks at home watching on black and white sets probably wondered what all the fuss was about.

On another occasion, thanks to a screwup by a technician, home viewers did get to see Spook showing his true colors. One of our sponsors was a now-defunct company called Big Bev Hamburgers. Spook's job— one he sometimes performed several times daily in our kitchen studio— was to take a huge bite out of a burger, quickly shift the food in his mouth so he could talk, and say, "Big Bev—it's delicious!"

Then, after a fade to black, the next image on the screen was supposed to be a cartoon. What viewers saw, thanks to the technician who accidentally cut back to the live commercial instead of forwarding to the show, was Spook's contorted face as he spit his Big Bev into the sink.

With the big money riding on commercial sponsors now, there's no telling what would have happened to Spook—not to mention the technician—if this type of flub-up happened today. But television was an infant in the 1950's, and most people were fairly relaxed about the new baby's growing pains. Besides, there weren't many viewers to witness these spectacles. When I started at WCMH in January of 1953, only about twelve to fifteen thousand Columbus-area homes were equipped with TV sets.

Maybe that's why so few people in the early days developed superstar-size egos. Something new and different was happening every day, and no matter how much experience we had in print and radio, we were all beginners when it came to television.

Working at the station was serious business, but it was also a lot of fun. Henry O'Neill, Dave Nichols, Bill Hindman and I were the station's four announcers, and each of us earned $87.50 for working seven days a week. Most of us did our best to behave professionally—most of the time. But, like Spook and his Big Bev burger episode, it wasn't unusual for the live camera to catch the humor behind the scenes.

Occasionally, it was at my expense. One incident that comes to mind involved Lex Mayers, an old fraternity brother of mine from Ohio University, who hosted a Friday night movie at the station. Lex's job did not require him to be a union member, and he wasn't permitted to do commercials, which were union-controlled. Since I had helped organize the Columbus/Dayton local of AFTRA and was a staunch union member (I was president for fourteen years), Lex asked me to be his announcer during commercial breaks.

In those days, car dealers didn't do their own ads. Instead, they'd wheel a couple of cars in, stick a fact sheet on the windshield and rely on the announcer to take it from there. I'd been off work for three weeks, recovering from a double hernia operation, and was actually looking forward to ad-libbing about the two cars the sponsor had sent over. I was taken aback, though, when I opened a car door before the show to check out the interior and the handle came off in my hand.

"Don't worry about that, Jim," Lex assured me. "We'll use that in your spiel—pull off the door handle again, and I'll say how easy it is to fix and that we'll knock $50 off the price of the car."

It sounded dumb to me but it was Lex's show and I wasn't going to tell him what to do. So when Lex cut to a commercial, I began describing the car and again pulled off the door handle. At that point, Lex changed his story. "Gee, Jim," he said. "I guess since you had that double hernia operation you just don't know your own strength." Oh, the hazards of live television! I was tempted to crawl under the car and disappear.

The Jack Pritchard situation was another boo-boo that involved a commercial, and it's one I witnessed firsthand a couple of weeks after signing on with WCMH. Another of our major sponsors was Eavey's Super-markets, whose products were pitched live by Amy Stafford in our kitchen studio. Rather than just telling viewers how great a particular product was, Amy did station break segments demonstrating various types of food preparation. Showing exactly what she was measuring, cutting or cooking often called for closeup camera shots. In those early days, closeups required manually moving the camera closer to the subject.

Jack, the cameraman, usually followed the instructions the director spoke into his headset without a hitch, treating viewers to a smooth, seemingly effortless closeup. One day, though, as Amy was preparing a potroast, the director inadvertently cracked Jack up and—as he shook with laughter—the camera jiggled, causing Amy and her potroast to jump all over the screen. Apparently his innocent directions hit Jack the wrong way. Instead of telling the cameraman to zoom in on the potroast, what the director said was, "Dolly in on Amy's meat." Whew! I was glad I had nothing to do with that one.

In most cases, I relied on cameramen mainly for studio work. I'd learned to use the heavy, bulky old cameras myself and—until the 1970's when union regulations barred anchors and reporters from doing their own filming—I usually shot my own film on location and also did my own editing back at the studio.

Editing film was definitely not high tech in those early days. It consisted of cutting out the unused portions of film, then using an emery board and glue to splice the two segments together. That's where the expression "winding up on the cutting room floor" comes from. Sometimes editing footage of a major sports event entailed making as many as five hundred splices. With all those cuts, it wasn't unusual for the film to break later when it was being run.

Still, despite the headaches involved, I enjoyed handling all the aspects of production—and it was definitely an advantage to be able to do everything myself. Knowing how to"shoot my own" came in handy when I was invited by the U.S. Trotting Association to go the the Hambletonian Classic, an annual harness race for three-year-old trotters. At that time, the race was held in Du Quoin, a town in southern Illinois.

I traveled from Columbus with a group of print journalists and members of the U.S. Trotting Association. We flew into St. Louis, then rented a car to drive to Du Quoin. These guys had a favorite watering hole in a little town called Red Bud, Illinois, so we stopped there for a beer.

The rest of the guys ordered Anheuser-Busch products, but because I was sponsored by Blatz Beer, I decided out of loyalty to order one. I took a lot of kidding but decided I'd educate them when the beer was served. "Do you serve much Blatz out here?" I asked the bartender, confident that it was a popular and superior product. "With that bottle I sold you, Mac, I just doubled my sales for the whole month," he replied. For the rest of the trip, the guys kidded me that I might know something about sports, but I sure as hell knew nothing about beer.

My interest in being a jack-of-all-trades paid off in the spring of 1956 when, three years after joining WCMH, I got permission from station executives to write and produce a series of hunting programs. We weren't going after Ohio game, though, and that's what made the project so exciting. Instead, I was given the go-ahead to organize an expedition to Kodiak Island, south of the Alaskan Penisula, to hunt the famed Kodiak bear, a huge brown animal that's indigenous to the island.

Our sponsors, lined up by Lloyd Forrest, the station's account executive, were Smith and Lee Sports, a sporting goods store in Grandview, and Big Bear Stores. In return for agreeing to mention them on the television series, we'd also gotten discounted rates from TWA and Northwest Airlines. Smith and Lee provided the Remington .300 H&H magnums and other hunting equipment, as well as fishing gear—including rods, reels, and bows and barbed fishing arrows for some exciting salmon fishing to round out the 30-day expedition.

As part of their sponsorship, Dick von Maur, a Smith and Lee owner, went with me and cameraman Denver Simmons on the trip. Our goal was to bring back one bear each and thousands of feet of film about the expedition for a 13-week series—the first locally-produced color series in Columbus television history.

Because hunting Kodiak bears is so dangerous, Alaskan law required every hunter to be accompanied by a registered guide. Our trip was so lengthy that two hunting guides, Oscar Nelson and Bill Poland, were with us for two weeks each because they had bookings with other hunters. After eight weeks of extensive preparation—hiring guides, getting together our equipment, convincing our wives that such a long trip really was necessary—Denver, Dick and I left Columbus on May 11, 1956 on the first leg of our Alaskan journey.

Today, a trip to Alaska may not seem particularly glamorous or perilous, but in 1956 it seemed as far away as the moon—and its nearly 600,000 square miles were thought to be about as desolate. This skepticism about Alaska dated back nearly 100 years to when the Secretary of State

William Seward bought the land from Russia in 1867. Although the government paid only about two cents an acre for the land, the seven million dollar purchase was popularly described as "Seward's folly."

It was 1959 before the country thought enough of the place to make it a state. With a population of less than 130,000 in the late 1950's when we made our trip, it was certainly the least sparsely settled. No wonder our expedition in the "Frozen North" was regarded as a wild and woolly adventure!

Getting to our destination was an adventure in itself. Unlike present-day flights to Alaska from the midwest, which usually take several hours and require one stop in Seattle, our actual flying time was twenty-one hours. After leaving Columbus, our plane stopped in Detroit, Milwaukee, Minneapolis, Spokane and Seattle before setting out for an overnight flight to Anchorage. A review of my "Big Bear Hunt" television scripts shows that I reported with great awe that the Northwest Airlines double-decker plane seated eighty-three passengers and reached a maximum cruising speed of 340 miles an hour.

My love affair with technology was dampened when we reached Anchorage and found our flights to Kodiak Island were cancelled because of a force more powerful than machines—Mother Nature. The rain and fog cleared after three days and we were able to fly on to Kodiak Island to put ourselves in the able hands of Oscar Nelson, our guide for the first half of the trip.

Besides needing his eighteen years of bear hunting experience, we also needed Oscar to help us carry four hundred pounds of equipment to his 42-foot boat. His boat served as our floating hotel during the weeks we spent with him circling Kodiak Island. Our belongings included hunting and fishing gear, a fifty-pound sound camera, three sixteen-millimeter movie cameras and 7,000 feet of color film. We'd need every ounce of this paraphernalia before the trip was over—especially the film, which was used to photograph seals, ducks and assorted other wildlife in addition to bears.

Because I was the smallest guy on board, I got the smallest bunk. That sounded fair enough—until I found out it was located in the engine room about twelve inches above the huge diesel engine. I soon grew accustomed to its low noise at night, but never got used to being jolted awake when Oscar punched it up to continue our trip each morning. This daily rush of adrenalin got my heart pumping in a big way. And later, when I did come within a stone's throw of some Kodiak bears, the juices really flowed.

Although it may seem strange to track bears from a boat, it was actually the most efficient way to sight the animals. Equipped with binoculars, Dick, Oscar and I scanned the island and, when we spotted some likely specimens, we took a small skiff ashore to continue tracking them on foot. To make a long and exciting story short, by the end of our trip we had gotten in many hours of salmon fishing and also bagged an eight-and-a-half foot, 1100-pound bear and a 10-foot, 1300-pound bear.

After it was stuffed by a taxidermist in Seattle, the larger bear stood for months in the lobby at the station. Later, because their team name is "Golden Bears," Dick von Maur donated it to Upper Arlington High School. Big Bear Stores got the smaller bear. The only mishap related to the whole adventure occurred months after we returned. Our building superintendent, Walter Postle, accidentally walked into the claws of the bear in our lobby and received cuts deep enough to require stitches.

To this day, I thank my patient wife, Miriam, for being such a great sport about my travels—particularly in regard to the Alaska trip, which kept me away from home longer than any other. Within a year after my return, our first child, Kelly, was born, a blessed event that made me even more reluctant to be away for extended periods.

But in the news business, long trips are sometimes necessary to cover distant events. And that was the case several years later in 1963 when the station sent me to cover the Pan American Games in Sao Paulo, Brazil, where Ohio State athletes Gary Bradds and Lou Vitucci were competing, accompanied by OSU trainer Ernie Biggs. Estelle Baskerville from East High School was also there, along with a synchronized swimming judge from Columbus. By this time, Jimmy Jr. had arrived, so I was doubly grateful to Miriam for her willingness to hold down the fort while I was away.

For this three-week trip I traveled alone, loaded down with even more paraphernalia than usual. In addition to a 16 mm silent camera, I carried an Auricon sound camera and 15,000 feet of black and white film from which to produce three half-hour shows about the games. Since the station could not have afforded to send two people, I was glad I'd learned to use all the equipment.

As it turned out, I was the only guy down there who wasn't from a major network. I'm sure my being a jack-of-all-trades was the main reason. The local stations simply could not afford to send two or three people halfway around the world, no matter how good the story was. So, even though dragging around all that equipment was no treat for a little short guy, the footage I got made lugging it worthwhile.

Although I was skilled at shooting film, conducting interviews, and all the other tasks related to producing a program, I was sadly lacking in foreign language skills. Like most Americans, my knowledge of Portuguese was zilch. But because the games draw an international crowd, I didn't think my inability to say anything beyond "yes," "no," "How much?" and "Where's the toilet?" would create any major difficulties.

What I didn't anticipate was all the things that are guaranteed to go wrong in a foreign country: Airline people who've never seen your luggage, cab drivers who've never seen your hotel, hotel people who've never seen your reservation. Toss in an inability to speak the native tongue and you're talking major problems. No wonder they called us "ugly Americans." There's nothing uglier than a basically good-natured tourist who's tired, frustrated, and longing for his toothbrush and a place to lay his head.

Amazing as it seems, all these problems were solved by a fellow Ohioan I ran into when the cabbie eventually delivered me to my hotel. Even more amazing was the fact that my savior was someone I knew— George Howser, a longtime friend from Marion, Ohio, who worked for the Marion Power and Shovel Company. George's job took him all over the world, and he was well-known in Sao Paulo and at the U.S. Embassy there. He got me checked in, tracked down my luggage and, through the Embassy, arranged for an interpreter to accompany me during my stay.

The interpreter's services proved to be invaluable. Through him, I learned that a Brazilian had purchased the exclusive rights to televise the Games and that he was charging ABC's "Wide World of Sports" $100,000 to shoot unlimited footage. Since I was from a local station, he told the interpreter he'd give me a break—for only $10,000 I could shoot 100 feet of film on each of the Ohio State athletes. This amounted to a total of only ten or fifteen minutes and, since I needed a few hours of film to edit down to three half-hour programs it wouldn't be nearly enough.

Besides, a phone call to the station confirmed what I already knew—they couldn't afford to pay the man anything, much less what he was asking. I was told to either find a free solution to the problem or come on home.

Meantime, while chatting with the Brazilian, my interpreter learned he was a fan of old movies and books who was looking for a hardback edition of *Gone with the Wind*. Because the interpreter promised to locate the book for him, he said he'd drop the price for filming from ten thousand dollars to one thousand dollars. This guy was obviously a wheeler and a dealer. It sounded like a bargain to me, so I again called the station. Because the man had promised me in writing the opportunity to shoot unlimited film footage of the Columbus folks, they agreed to wire the money.

The only hitch was that the Brazilian made me promise to shoot film only of the Ohio competitors. The interpreter made it clear that the man was deadly serious about this stipulation. In fact, I was told he had threatened to destroy all my film if I so much as turned the camera on anyone else for a second. I took "anyone" to mean the other athletes and was surprised later when the interpreter became upset after I took a quick cutaway shot of the Brazilian's cameraman filming the events. He convinced me to confess right away that I'd taken a shot of the cameraman, saying the man would become even more enraged if he found out later.

As we trudged back to admit to my "crime," I felt sure it was all over. All my efforts were going to go unrewarded and I'd have to return to the States emptyhanded. I wasn't surprised when the Brazilian immediately demanded the contract and took it back to his inner office. We heard the sound of ripping paper and my heart sank.

Then we heard the sound of a typewriter and within a few minutes the man came out with yet another contract. This one gave me unlimited filming rights for a mere one $100—precisely $99,900 dollars less than the networks paid for the privilege. Needless to say, I was flabbergasted—both before and after the interpreter explained the Brazilian's motives. It seems the name of the man's company, "Amplivision," was on the side of his cameras. He was thrilled that I had chosen to show his company's name in the United States, if only for two or three seconds.

The whole experience taught me an old but valuable lesson: Never look a gift horse in the mouth, no matter what language he speaks. I took the new contract and got out of there before he changed his mind.

Another situation in Brazil that related to language drove home to me the importance of knowing social customs when traveling abroad. I had heard that the word *abrigato* in Portuguese meant thank you, and that *muyto abrigato* meant "thank you very much." So to show the old man I bought a daily paper from how extremely polite I was, I'd say "*muyto abrigato*" to him each day when I bought the English language newspaper. He never answered in words, but instead responded with a big, beautiful and nearly toothless smile.

When I got back to the states I learned that *abrigato* is acceptable anytime, but *muyto abrigato* is a phrase reserved for people you love. Oops!

Since covering the Pan Am Games thirty years ago I've had bigger budgets, fancier equipment, and easier assignments. But I can't remember when I've had quite as much fun.

3

A Friend Named Woody

It was one of those snowy football practices that Woody called a "two T-shirt day"—so miserably cold that it was difficult for the players to concentrate. I was there watching from the sidelines with Kaye Kessler, an old friend who for years covered Ohio State for the old *Columbus Citizen Journal*. Although Woody closed his practices to the public, he did allow reporters to observe on the condition that we stay out of the way and keep our mouths shut.

As always, Woody ignored the weather and expected his players to do the same. He was a "hands on" coach both literally and figuratively, who had a habit of getting right down in the huddle with his players and calling the plays. Then when the boys would get up to the line of scrimmage, Woody would stay on the field and watch the action.

On this day in the early 1960's, the first thing that happened was that a big fullback hit the line and got creamed. Right away, Woody was on him with an instant correction, which was his style of coaching. "God dammit!" Woody shouted, as he grabbed the kid's shoulder pads and kicked him in the rear. "How many time to do I have to tell you, before you run—think, think, think!"

The kid nodded and the players went back into the huddle, where Woody called the same play. Again, the fullback got creamed. This time, Woody went up to him, grabbed his shoulder pads, hit him on the helmet and yelled, "How many times do I have to tell you, don't think—just run, run, run!"

On the sidelines, Kaye Kessler and I were laughing so hard that we momentarily forgot the cold—we were watching classic Woody Hayes and loving every minute. I couldn't help thinking of the famous line from Woody's favorite philosopher, Ralph Waldo Emerson: "A foolish consistency is the hobgoblin of small minds." Regardless of the other things they said about him, few people accused Woody of having a small mind.

Woody had an opinion about everything and he was never shy about sharing it with the world. He majored in history and English at Denison, graduating in 1935, and was a history buff all his life. He was particularly well read on military strategy and General George Patton was his hero.

I never saw anyone who could out-talk Woody when it came to discussing war. Once, early in my career, I went to hear a speech Woody gave at Lockbourne Air Force Base—now Rickenbacker Air National Guard Base—when it was still part of the Strategic Air Command. General Curtis E. LeMay, commander of the SAC, had invited Woody to speak to a roomful of the top brass. I was asked to introduce Woody, and having been only a corporal in the Marines, I was more than a little intimidated by this high-level group.

Woody, however, looked no more nervous than he would have at a football rally—maybe because he'd been the commander of a Navy ship and had a few ribbons of his own. He immediately captured their attention with an off-the-cuff speech about the similarities between his military experience and his coaching career, including what his strategy would be in war versus his strategy on the football field. Even though he spoke for more than an hour, the audience's attention never wavered.

As I listened to his speech, I recalled something Kaye Kessler once wrote in his column: If you don't want to like Woody Hayes, don't listen to him speak. Kessler was right—the man was mesmerizing. That roomful of military honchos must have thought so, too. They gave him a standing ovation.

Although within a few years he was able to build a reputation both as a public speaker and a coach, few people knew Woody when he was hired by Ohio State in 1951. Coincidentally, that was my also first year reporting on OSU football for WRFD Radio in Worthington—one of my many part-time broadcast jobs while I was a student at Ohio University. Woody was fifteen years my senior, but I like to think we grew up together professionally over the following thirty years. Certainly neither of us was well known at the time.

I remember the newspaper headlines of "Woody Who?" when he came to Ohio State from Miami University in Oxford, Ohio, where he'd coached from 1949 to 1951. Before that he'd been Denison's coach for three years. Until he took the Denison job in 1946, Woody had been a high school coach and history teacher in the small Ohio towns of Mingo Junction and New Philadelphia. Along the way he'd earned a master's degree from Ohio State in educational administration with the idea of possibly becoming a school superintendent like his dad had been.

Moving up to coach at a Big Ten school was a major step forward for Woody, and he knew it. He also knew he wasn't Ohio State's first choice. Don Faurot of Missouri had already turned the job down—probably for reasons of self-preservation. Ohio State was known in the early fifties as the graveyard of coaches, and for good reason. After Francis Schmidt, who coached from 1928 until 1940 when he was fired after a 40-0 loss to Michigan, Paul Brown took the job. Brown was a popular choice, having coached the Massillon Tigers to six straight Ohio champion-ships. Three years later, after a couple of good seasons followed by a dismal 1943 when he lost most of his best players to the military, Brown joined the Navy himself.

Carroll Widdoes, an assistant coach, took over until 1945 when he resigned after a loss to Michigan. Widdoes was replaced by Wes Fesler, a former All-American at Ohio State, who in 1947 made Big Ten history by being the first coach to lead the Buckeyes to a last place finish. Fesler hung in there until he was forced to resign after a loss to Michigan in the famous 1950 "Blizzard Bowl," when—thanks to Athletic Director Dick Larkins' decision not to postpone the game—the teams played through the worst snowstorm to hit Ohio in nearly 40 years.

Temperatures dropped to five above zero and 40 mile-an-hour winds lashed the stadium, but 50,000 fans still turned out to watch the wolverines take a 9-3 victory on field covered with four inches of snow. Astoundingly, the bands performed at half-time, but their music was swept away by howling winds. Many out-of-town fans were stranded in Columbus for several days after the game, and the university was closed for four days the following week.

The turnout for the Blizzard Bowl probably did more than any other single event to convince the rest of the country that Columbus was truly a football crazy town—especially since this devotion occurred at the end of a dismal season that featured six losses, a tie and only two wins. For the first time in Buckeye history, Ohio State was in the Western Conference cellar. Fans wanted Paul Brown to come back and take over his old job, and there was a big movement in Columbus called "BBB" for Bring Back Brown. But he had left college ball and, as the world knows, went on to make quite a name for himself coaching the Cleveland Browns.

Woody's name had been put in the hopper by his master's thesis adviser, and he more or less got the job by default when Faurot turned it down. The other candidates were cautious about carving their own professional tombstones at a school that chewed up coaches.

In his typically optimistic way, rather than feeling hurt because he wasn't first choice, Woody saw it as an advantage. Here's how he explained it in his 1973 book, *You Win With People*: "Not being at the top of the list gave me an advantage because I was not subject to the criticism and barbs that a front runner invariably experiences. I made up my mind to one thing—that in a distance race a dark horse can put on a sprint only once if he expects to win, so he must be ready when his time comes."

No one knew better than Woody that his time had come—it was just that the rest of the world hadn't realized it. He'd had a good record at Denison and Miami, but in the Big Ten he certainly wasn't well known. Anyone looking at his first season results wouldn't have expected him to have lasted much longer than some of his predecessors. Woody himself described the 1951 season as "at best, mediocre." Under Woody's tutelage the Buckeyes did win their first game that season, beating SMU 7-0. But they were beaten by Michigan State, Indiana and Michigan and wound up with a 4-3-2 record.

Woody's second and third years were better, with identical records both years: six wins—including a 27-7 victory over Michigan in 1952—and three losses. The big win over Michigan in 1952 was turned around the following year when the Wolverines whipped the Bucks 20-0.

It was rumored after the first season that Ernie Godfrey, an assistant coach at Ohio State since 1929, was asked by Athletic Department administrators to replace Woody. Godfrey flatly turned down the offer saying, "No, Woody is my boss." Another rumor had it that a group of wealthy fans wanted to buy out the remainder of Woody's three-year contract—which was actually more of a gentleman's agreement—so the university could replace him.

If Woody was concerned about any of these rumblings, he didn't let on. Throughout his career, one of his favorite comments was, "I'm not here to win popularity contests—I'm here to win football games." But of course Woody was aware of public opinion. He used to tell the story of being out in his yard on a quiet summer evening before the 1954 season and overhearing a neighbor's house guest say Ohio State should get rid of Woody Hayes. Woody's response was to get up an hour earlier every day so he could devote even more time to building a winning team. It was this attitude that won him the well-deserved reputation as the hardest working coach in college football.

Woody's sensible attitude toward public opinion enabled him to devote his emotional energy to the game instead of toward stewing about what people thought—a lesson some who followed him never learned. In these early years, Woody was busy building a team and teaching his players and assistant coaches his brand of football which, because it was based on a running offense, was popularly known as "three yards and a cloud of dust."

All Woody's hard work paid off in 1954. The Bucks had eight wins and no losses when they faced Michigan in the season's final game. The Associated Press had named them number one in the nation and it was clear that Woody had put together a great team: Howard "Hopalong" Cassady, Dave Leggett, Hubert Bobo, Jim Parker and Dick Brubaker, to name just a few.

The 1954 game against Michigan that won them the Big Ten title was the greatest game I've ever seen Ohio State play. The Wolverines got a quick 7-0 lead but the Bucks tied the game in the second quarter. The most amazing action occurred early in the fourth quarter when Michigan was stopped on the six inch line by the entire Ohio State team. Woody always described this as the greatest goal line stand he'd ever seen and I have to agree. In that last quarter, the Buckeyes steamrollered Michigan for a 21-7 win that brought them the National Championship.

The victory over Michigan also closed out an incredible season. Thanks to Woody's coaching and the efforts of his talented players, for the first time in 41 years a Western Conference team ended the season with a perfect record. The historic win over Michigan was followed by a rainy, muddy 20-7 Rose Bowl victory over Southern California. At the end of this season, no one in Columbus—or anywhere else in the United States—would ever again ask that annoying question, "Woody who?"

For the next twenty-five years Woody would more often than not be the center of one storm or another—storms the media reported in great detail and with great enthusiasm. Woody had gotten off on the wrong foot with the press practically from the beginning, when he refused to let reporters covering the 1955 Rose Bowl game conduct a pre-game interview with his players. Afterwards, he kept the press waiting and gave what many described as a less than gracious interview. As a result, throughout his career he had a rocky relationship with the California media.

Other stories of his treatment of the press are legion: how he once kicked a reporter out of a press conference for using a tape recorder, only to give him an exclusive interview later when he returned with a notebook to record the conversation; the time he threw out an entire contingent of reporters covering a preseason drill because the team was doing poorly; the 1973 Rose Bowl incident when he lunged at an *LA Times* photographer who was illegally on the field, jamming the camera into the man's face and bruising his eye.

Most reporters who covered him eventually had a run-in with Woody, though not necessarily a physical one. Mine came after a game at Ohio Stadium against Minnesota. Although the Bucks won, they were doing poorly in the first half and Woody was incensed. He'd already ripped up his hat and thrown down his glasses a few times. I was shooting game footage from the sidelines and a photographer for *The Lantern,* Ohio

State's student newspaper, was standing beside me. Each time Woody threw a tantrum, the kid held up his camera to frame a perfect shot.

Having his rages photographed made Woody even madder. Before the start of the second half he marched up to the young photographer, stuck his finger right up in the kid's face and shouted,"You take one more picture of me and I'll ram that camera down your throat." Naturally, the kid was terrified and quit taking pictures.

At the news conference following the game I asked Woody, "Since when is it ethical for you to do what you did to that poor kid today?" Woody jumped up and said, "It's my goddam stadium and I'll do whatever I want to."

I was too mad myself to back off, so I shot back with, "I think your behavior was bush league." This criticism was too much for Woody—he jumped up and started after me. If sports reporter Dick Otte hadn't gotten between us to head Woody off, I'm convinced there would have been some blood shed. For the next six months, Woody made a point of ignoring me. I'd be at Ohio State interviewing some of the other coaches, and Woody would say hello to everyone but me.

This *persona non grata* treatment continued until I ran into Woody one night sitting alone at the counter of a local restaurant where I often went for a cup of coffee. When I asked if he minded if I joined him, he replied as though nothing had ever happened, "Come on and sit down, Jim, I haven't seen you in some time."

"The hell you haven't," I replied. "I've seen you quite often since football season but you haven't spoken to me. Am I still on your list?" Woody jutted out his jaw and said, "Goddammit, Jim, I still don't agree with what you said in the locker room that day, but, goddammit, I give you credit for having the guts to say it."

From that point on—although we'd have our differences over the years—Woody and I began a friendship built on mutual respect. We also had many laughs together, sometimes at his expense and sometimes at mine.

When my daughter Kelly was about three years old, she got a real belly laugh out of Woody. Kelly and my wife, Miriam, were waiting for me in the Channel 4 lobby after I did a live, 30-minute show with Woody and Ohio's top high school football players. I'd already told Woody about how Kelly watched his weekly show faithfully on WBNS-TV Thursday at 6 p.m. instead of watching me on WCMH on that evening.

I knew that Kelly, who called him Woody "Hayve," would be thrilled to see her hero in person. "Let's see if Kelly recognizes you." I whispered to Woody as we walked into the lobby.

When we got right in front of her, I said, "Kelly, do you know who this is?" "Woody Hayve!" she replied, all happy and bright-eyed—whereupon Woody picked her up and began chatting with her.

Kelly looked him over in a friendly way, then reached down and patted his stomach. "Woody Hayve have a big fat tummy!" she announced cheerfully. Woody exploded with laughter. "Anne's [Mrs. Hayes] been telling me that for a long time," he said, "but it took a three-year-old to get the point across." For the rest of his life, Kelly was one of Woody's favorites; he was at her wedding in January 1985.

Kelly was one of hundreds of children that Woody kept in touch with. He was always available to go with me to Children's Hospital and visit patients, or to provide signed photographs for me to give the many children who worshiped him. Woody had gotten involved in community service long before we became friends, but "Woody the humanitarian" was a private role, one he didn't want outsiders to see.

Shortly after he moved his office into the Ernie Biggs Athletic Facility, I noticed an erector set on a shelf when I dropped by. It was only after I kidded him about being in his second childhood that he told me he was taking it to a little boy at University Hospital. When I asked who it was, Woody said he didn't know, just that he'd heard there was a young football fan who needed cheering up. Then he warned me that I'd better not breathe a word about it to anyone.

Only after he retired was Woody willing to publicly show this soft side of himself. In fact, he rarely got through a speech in his later years without tears standing in his eyes. This emotional behavior shocked a lot of people, but those of us who knew him well weren't surprised. Beneath his tough exterior, Woody was a kind and thoughtful man, and a very loyal one—especially to his players and their families.

Back in the 1950's, Hop Cassady's son, David, was struck by a car in Detroit, where his dad was playing pro football for the Lions. When Woody learned of the accident, he went behind the scenes to several wealthy people and asked them to match his thousand dollar donation to help Hop defray his son's medical expenses. "We owe this to Hop for what he gave Ohio State," he told them. Everyone he approached made a contribution.

David Cassady, by the way, is now in his thirties. As a result of brain damage suffered from the accident, he's partially paralyzed and has a speech impediment. A delightful man, David has come to our Recreation Unlimited camps for many years. At the time, Kaye Kessler and I went to Woody's office to see if the rumor about his fundraising for David was true. We both felt it would have been a great human interest piece for his column and my commentary. Woody immediately shot down our idea. He reluctantly confirmed the story—then threatened to kill us if we ran an article.

Nearly all his former players, from superstars like 1974-75 Heisman trophy recipient Archie Griffin to hundreds of other less famous people, have similar "Woody stories" that illustrate the remarkably generous side of his character. Many of them will also tell you that it was only after graduation, when the fear wore off, that they appreciated what "the old man" had done for them.

His staff also loves to reminisce about Woody. In 1988 I talked about Woody with George Hill, formerly Woody's defensive coordinator, and at that time defensive coordinator for the Indianapolis Colts. I was in town to cover a sports event, and George and I naturally got to talking about Woody over lunch. George recalled an incident that happened in 1975, following a 21 to 14 win over Michigan.

Woody had been greeted by a woman who presented him with twenty-one red roses when the team returned to the Port Columbus airport. As they left the airport, Woody told George to meet him at 11 p.m. at the television studio to prepare for the Woody Hayes show at 11:30 p.m. that night. George was there promptly, but Woody didn't show up until 11:20.

When George asked where he'd been, Woody said he'd been at University Hospital dividing up the roses among a group of elderly patients. Of course, he'd chatted with each one and that's had what thrown off his schedule. "There are little old ladies in that hospital, George, who are worried about whether they're going to live or die,"

Woody explained. "And all we're worried about is a damned football game. I think I did something today to make some people happy."

Off the field, Woody's kindness helped him put the game into perspective. On the field, the enormous strength of his personality was directed toward the game. When it came to his players, Woody was a master psychologist and his biggest weapon was intimidation, but it was intimidation with a purpose. Moose Machinsky, captain of the 1957 team, told me his performance was motivated by fear of what would happen if he missed a play on the field or a class assignment off it. Woody pushed his players—often literally pounding on them—to become the best they could be. In return, they feared him, respected him and—when they matured enough to appreciate what he was up to—loved him.

But because they saw only the tough guy side, plenty of outsiders disliked Woody and went out of their ways to let him know it through nasty phone calls, letters, and heckling at games. One "cheer" that was popular for a while was, "Oh, come let's sing Ohio's praise/And say good-bye to Woody Hayes." It undoubtedly irritated Woody, but he ignored it all. In his mind, responding to pressure would have been a sign of giving in.

For example, despite the fact that having a listed phone number left him open to constant harassment, it went against Woody's principles to remove his name from the phone directory. The phone rang off the hook on football Saturdays and midnight calls from angry fans were a regular occurrence. But Woody refused to surrender what he saw as his right to have a listed number. Even today, there's a listing in the Columbus directory for W.W. Hayes on the quiet street near campus where his his wife, Anne, still lives in the home they bought in 1951.

This dedication to principle was typical of Woody, a rock-ribbed conservative who visited Viet Nam several times during an unpopular war that tore apart Ohio State and other campuses. The fact that many of his players, most of the professors and nearly everyone else on campus had a strong anti-war bias didn't stop Woody from sticking by his beliefs.

Not surprisingly, the students respected him for it. On a spring day in 1970 when five thousand war protestors massed on Ohio State's Oval— some armed with rocks and bricks—and were confronted by 1,200 armed police and National Guardsmen, Woody's was one of the few voices of reason that students were willing to listen to. During the thirteen-day student strike, he was able to talk with small groups of students and defuse a very volatile situation. Later, many students and university officials credited Woody with helping Ohio State avert a senseless tragedy like the one that occurred at Kent State.

The respect Woody got from students paled in comparison to the way young GI's felt about him. Shortly after Woody's death I received a letter from a former service man who had met Woody in Viet Nam. The letter, signed simply "a face in the crowd" speaks movingly of the real Woody Hayes.

"Some 20 years ago, I drew the short straw. Someone had to guard a nameless patch of dirt that neither we nor the V.C. cared about. Late in the afternoon I heard a raspy voice bellow out my name—it was Woody.

"The story goes that the USO troupe met with some officers after the performance and Woody asked if there were any Ohio boys who hadn't been able to make the show. My CO told him about me, and when Woody learned he would be passing near he asked to stop and meet me. This idea was rejected by my CO because I was not in a safe zone. Woody twisted some general's arm and my CO was overruled.

"Since Woody's chopper had to be in a safe zone before nightfall, we briefly yelled at each other over the clatter of his helicopter. As the crew chief of the chopper motioned for Woody to get on board, he took out his pen and started to sign a photo of that year's OSU team. His pen was dry and I didn't have one. He yelled 'Come see me when you get home and I'll finish signing the picture.'

"It took me three years to get to his office. By then, I was in my second year at Ohio State. Many times before I had started to call or go in, but I figured he would be too busy or would not recall his offer of a photograph. The day I finally did go, he wasn't there but his secretary took my name and home phone number and said she'd give Woody the message.

"That evening when I arrived home, Woody was sitting at the kitchen table talking with my wife. He stayed for dinner and both of us grew to know and love the real Woody Hayes. The times I saw Woody after that he asked about my wife by name and offered his help in various ways without strings or qualifications.

"Woody went out of his way to say hi to a grunt in Viet Nam. He made a special trip across town to sign a dog-eared picture of one of his earlier

teams. He turned a meal of macaroni and cheese into a feast my wife and I will never forget.

"Woody knew the faces in the crowd as well as those of the great and famous. That is why he will always be the greatest, the most notable and the all around best."

I'll always treasure that eloquent, anonymous letter because it shows the level of respect that Woody received for his treatment of his fellow man. Of course he also won widespread respect—even awe—for his performance as a coach. In the Block O section of Ohio Stadium reserved for students, a much-photographed sign posted during the turbulent 1960's declared, "God is alive and coaching at OSU."

With a career record of 238 wins, Woody could claim more victories than any coach except Alabama's Bear Bryant. Five times he led the Bucks to Rose Bowl victories: in 1955, 1958, 1969, 1971 and 1973. He was twice named college coach of the year, in 1957 and 1975. Fifty-eight of Woody's players were named All-Americans and three won Heisman trophies. Few would argue the fact that his talent, hard work and determination had made Wayne Woodrow Hayes a hero.

There was a dark side to this heroism, though, and it proved to be his downfall. Woody's temper was always bubbling just beneath the surface, ready to explode in frequent tirades or, less often, in violence. Throughout his career, this physical side would periodically erupt and get him into trouble. Two years before the famous Gator Bowl incident that ended his career in 1979, he was put on a year's probation by the Big Ten for slugging an ABC cameraman.

Woody's staff saw that he was beginning to lose control more frequently but they felt helpless to do anything about it. George Chaump, one of Woody's assistant coaches, told me after Woody's firing, "Winning was always an obsession with Woody. On the field and in the locker room we sensed he was at the point where he was going to lose control. All the coaches hoped it would be on the practice field and not in a game."

As the world knows, Woody's final loss of control happened on national television at the 1979 Gator Bowl. With a minute and fifty-eight seconds left on the clock, he slugged Clemson's Charlie Baumann after Baumann was forced out of bounds following his interception of an Ohio State pass. When one of his own players tried to subdue him, Woody continued to vent his rage by beating on the man's face mask. Early the next morning, to no one's surprise, Ohio State President Harold Enarson fired Woody Hayes.

Later that same day I received a call at home from Senator John Glenn, asking if I had seen Woody. I told him no, that the blinds were drawn at Woody's house, the doors locked and—for the first time I could recall—the phone was off the hook. We chatted for a few minutes and Senator Glenn asked me to tell Woody to call him collect in Washington. "Woody needs his friends right now," he said. "You know, Jimmy, we all make mistakes we'd like to correct. Woody's problem is that when he makes a mistake it's on national television in front of eighty million people. For that reason, everyone thinks he's a rotten old man, but we know better."

I think Senator Glenn's statement is a perfect summation of the Gator Bowl incident. True to form, as far as I know Woody never discussed the events leading to his firing with anyone outside his family. After a period of withdrawal, he resumed his attendance at football games in the role of spectator and also became a popular public speaker, both on and off campus.

During those first few years following his firing, Woody's health was good. He appeared to have made a complete recovery from the heart attack he had suffered in June, 1974. By all appearances, he was enjoying a healthy old age. But in 1985, when he was seventy-two, his health began a sharp decline. In May he suffered a stroke, followed by an angina attack in June and a mild heart attack that September.

When he was coaching, Woody had always told people he'd never retire. He vowed instead that he'd die on the fifty yard line at Ohio Stadium in front of eighty-seven thousand fans. Instead, death stole in and took him quietly. On March 12, 1987, Woody passed away in his sleep, apparently of a heart attack.

Knowing Woody, I'll bet he was outraged at the gall of his final opponent. "Damn you, death," he would have shouted, "for sneaking in like a coward instead of giving me notice to prepare for one last fight."

4

♦

Buckeye Basketball,
Taylor-Style

I am the first to admit that I aroused strong feelings, good and bad, among fans during the twenty years from 1959 to 1979 that I covered Ohio State basketball. There was the letter mailed in 1961 after the Buckeyes were whipped by Cincinnati in the NCAA finals. Addressed to "Ohio's Biggest Crumb, Columbus, Ohio," it was delivered directly to me.

And I thought the mission of the U.S. Postal Service was "Neither rain nor sleet or dark of night" will delay the mail! Apparently, personal insults don't hold it up either. Among other things, the Cincy fan had written, "Cincinnati 71, OSU, 59—how about that!"

The last part was a slam on an expression that has become so much a part of my sports talk repertoire that I decided to use it as the title for this book. I can still recall the first time I said it.

It was before an Ohio State-Indiana game in 1960, and I'd watched Fred Taylor walk his players through an offense that he'd diagrammed on the chalkboard. When they later ran the offense during the game, the team executed it perfectly. I was so excited that what I wanted to say would have gotten us thrown off the air. So I just shouted, "Howwww about that!"

Ouch! Having that thrown back at me in a letter the following year hurt. It was meant as a jab. I laughed, but I felt it—even though I probably had said "How about that!" a few hundred times in the interim. But I've never claimed to be Shakespeare, and that's why one of my favorite press clips is a defense of my reporting style that appeared as an editorial in the *Mt. Vernon News* in 1971. Here's what the Mt. Vernon reporter had to say:

"What critics should realize is that Jim has created a new art in sports reporting—that of the unsupported exclamatory phrase. Who can forget his supreme achievement in the Michigan game after a tip-in? 'Luke Witte was Johnny-on-the-spot, like a peanut butter and jelly sandwich at high noon.'

"Doesn't that draw a word picture for you? . . . They may love Chick Hearn who announces for the Los Angeles Lakers and Curt Gowdy may draw raves for his network descriptions, but let there be no more criticism of central Ohio's own Jimmy Crum. After all, look how far he's brought Fred Taylor! How about THAT, sports fans?"

The "up" side of being associated with that phrase was exemplified by an experience I'll never forget. It happened in 1961, the year after Taylor's team won the NCAA Championship. The team lost the championship to Cincinnati in 1961, but a ceremony was planned at St. John Arena. It was a great team and the kids had all worked their hearts out.

About ten thousand people had assembled at St. John for the ceremony when I arrived with Hugh DeMoss, who was then Channel 4's news director, and our photographer, Bobby Livingston. As we were setting up before the team got there, Bobby discovered he'd left a piece of equipment in the the car. Bobby Livingston wore a wooden leg, one he'd earned in World War II at Guadalcanal. He got around on his leg quite well, but we were in a rush and I offered to run out and get the equipment for him.

When I returned, I cut straight across the basketball court. I'd gotten about halfway across when someone way up in the top seats yelled, "How about that, sports fans!" The crowd picked it up and by the time I got across the floor to Bobby and Hugh, ten thousand fans were applauding me and yelling that phrase. "You son of a gun," DeMoss said, "you've got tears in your eyes!" It was one of those once-in-a-lifetime moments.

I also appreciated the praise from the *Mt. Vernon News*. Of course, the line about my bringing Fred Taylor along certainly wasn't the case, because Fred didn't need "bringing along" by anyone. Like Woody Hayes, he was and is highly respected as a coach and as a man. Fred became Ohio State's varsity basketball coach in 1958, the year before I started doing play-by-play coverage for WCMH-TV.

The station received the contract to cover Ohio State basketball for the next twenty years, until Channel 6 outbid us by a few thousand dollars in 1979. Channel 4 was the first station in town to televise OSU basketball, which at the time was remarkably affordable.

During those years, I was known as "the voice of Ohio State basketball" and I developed quite a following among fans. One was *Chicago Tribune* syndicated columnist and author Bob Greene, who in the early 1960's was a student at Bexley High School in Columbus.

At that time, Bob was a young teen-age basketball fan who happened to have season tickets that placed him right behind the scoring desk where my statistician, Gary Taylor (who was no relation to Fred) and I sat in St. John Arena. Bob and Gary got to talking one night and Bob volunteered to help Gary keep stats during the games.

Thirty years ago, there were no calculators or computers to track statistics. It was strictly a paper and pencil task and statisticians had to be quick, alert, and good at math to keep track of rebounds, scoring percentages, and so forth. Gary was happy to give Bob a chance to help out, especially since he did it for free.

When I compared the stats Bob gave me at half-time with the official statistics supplied at the end of the games, I found he was very close on all of them. I began to mention his name at every game, crediting Bob Greene and Gary Taylor with the statistics I was quoting. Bob became an important part of our team and worked with us for a few years until he graduated from high school.

Bob said he got a kick out of going into school on Monday morning and hearing the kids at Bexley High say they'd heard me talking about him on television. I don't know what kind of student Bob was—he was a smart kid so I assume he was average or above. But I do know that math wasn't his best subject.

I remember once he told me his dad said, "Jimmy was praising you last night on television about how close your half-time stats were to the official statistics. What I can't figure out is how you can get those figures so close when you're practically failing math!"

Bob was an absolute gem to work with. He wouldn't have cared whether we mentioned him at half-time or not. He went off to college at Northwestern and I lost touch with him until three years ago, when I invited him to Columbus to participate in our annual Celebrity Waiters' Luncheon to raise money for Recreation Unlimited.

When Bob learned all four of Ohio State's Heisman trophy winners— Les Horvath, Vic Janowicz, Hop Cassady, and Archie Griffin—would be waiters also, he was thrilled. Despite his own fame as a journalist, he was still in awe of these guys, and especially wanted to meet Hop Cassady.

Bob Greene's long memory is typical of sports fans. One of them proved this a few years ago while I was waiting in line at a crowded Red Lobster Restaurant out on Hamilton Road. This fellow trotted up to shake my hand and bellowed, "Hi, there, Jim. It's good to see you! Don't you remember me?" I stood back and studied him a minute. He had that southeastern Ohio drawl and I thought maybe I'd known him when I was in Athens at Ohio University. "No, sir," I finally admitted. "I'm afraid I can't place you."

"It was in St. John Arena in 1960 when Lucas and Havlicek were playing basketball," he insisted loudly. "You were standing at the urinal next to me and we talked about the team." Naturally, everyone around us cracked up. To this day, I shy away from conversations in men's rooms.

Not everyone was a fan, of course. An incident I do recall that occurred during the 1959-60 season when Ohio State won the NCAA Basketball Championship illustrates this point. I had covered a game televised during the Christmas holidays, and afterwards attended a Christmas party with my wife. The Bucks had won, of course, and it had been a close and exciting game. Like everyone else at St. John Arena that night, I felt wonderful—until I arrived at the party.

The hostess greeted Miriam pleasantly at the front door, then tore into me like a buzz saw. "You have absolutely ruined my Christmas party with that basketball game," she yelled. "All the men went into one room and watched TV and just ignored us women." I told her I was sorry, then Miriam and I promptly left. I knew the men would want to rehash the game with me, and I didn't think the disposition of the hostess was likely to improve.

Usually, though, my association with Ohio State basketball was a pleasant one. One of my favorite jobs was hosting "The Fred Taylor Show." Between covering the games and hosting the show, I got to know Fred quite well.

Fred's an Ohio boy who grew up in Zanesville and went on to graduate in 1950 from Ohio State, where he played center on one of the best-ever Buckeye teams. During his senior year, the Bucks had a 22-4 season—a record until ten years later when Fred coached the team to a 25-3 season and the NCAA championship. That team was so outstanding that the 1959-1960 season was described by the press as "the year of the Buckeyes."

Center Jerry Lucas, forwards John Havlicek and Joe Roberts, and guards Larry Siegfried and Mel Nowell deserved every bit of praise they received. This group of Ohio natives led by Lucas, became the nation's top scorers, hitting nearly 50 percent on field goals. The 6'8" Lucas had been the country's top high school scorer, wracking up 2,460 points to break Wilt Chamberlain's 2,252 point record set at a Philadelphia high school.

Lucas was a straight shooter off the court as well. An "A" student majoring in business, Lucas—who'd turned down athletic scholarships at other schools—carried a full course load and was proud that he was attending Ohio State on an academic scholarship.

Lucas was a serious guy and very much a team player. He was also the most unselfish player I've ever seen. I remember his coming into the locker room after games and looking up how many rebounds he got, not how many points he scored.

Lucas' teammates were also an impressive group. Larry Siegfried was the Bucks' leading scorer in 1958-59, averaging nearly 20 points a game as a sophomore. Like Lucas, Siegfried had also been a top high school scorer, averaging 38 points a game. Under Fred's coaching, he sublimated his desire to be an offense star and, teamed with Columbus native Mel Nowell, became an unbelievably tough guard his last two seasons. He still managed to be the team's second leading scorer.

Forward John ("Hondo") Havlicek also figured into Fred's emphasis on defense. An all-state high school athlete in football and baseball as well as basketball, Havlicek once told a reporter that if team members had tried to score individually as they had in high school, the board would have shown 150 points a game.

"I knew that wasn't going to happen," he said, "so I forgot about the offense because I knew that concentrating on defense was the quickest way to make the team." John Havlicek's patience was rewarded—he later got his chance to shoot for the Celtics and became the fourth leading scorer in NBA history.

Joe Roberts, another tall (6'7") and talented member of that famous team, was a fine forward and an aggressive player who unselfishly and repeatedly set Lucas up to shoot. Roberts played pro ball for four years after his stint with the Buckeyes. Although he was not one of the five starters on the 1960 team, Dick Furry was another excellent forward who got a lot of play. Also on that famous team was Bobby Knight who, while not a star player, showed a lot of hustle.

A lot of people—none of them coaches—have said that with this kind of talent, Fred's job was a cinch, with the championship all but locked up from the outset. Nothing could have been further from the truth. What he could have wound up with was a bunch of talented hot dogs, all out for their own glory. What he shaped was a team that worked as a unit, that put the larger goal of unselfishly working together ahead of their own egos. How many supposedly mature adults can make that claim?

Like Woody Hayes, Fred Taylor did everything in his power to see that his players graduated. He was not a "user" who saw these kids only as finely-tuned athletes whose sole purpose was to bring glory to Ohio State. Fred was very realistic, and urged his players to be realistic, about their chances of turning pro.

He often reminded even his most talented players that only a handful of college stars each year were selected by the pro teams. "The odds are not very good that you'll make it," he told them bluntly. "If you don't get your degree while doing something you enjoy, then it isn't worth it to you." To his credit, all Fred's players graduated.

Fred's practices were usually open to the public, and back in the early 1960's during the championship years, he'd sometimes have 1,500 fans turn out. It was a joy to watch Fred work with those kids. There was a big, broad-shouldered guy named Walt Bellamy who played center for Indiana, and I loved watching Fred diagram on the blackboard what the team was going to do to stop Bellamy. He'd get the players out on the floor one on one, then two on two and walk them through it. He'd have them practice it half court, then full court. Fred would put them through it over and over again. When we saw it in the game it was like a well-rehearsed stage play. Fred Taylor taught his players a beautiful execution of both offense and defense.

I spent many pleasant hours talking with Fred and his teams during the years I hosted "The Fred Taylor Show." Our set was a round stage made up of two big half-moons that fit together to look like a big basketball when the camera shot it from overhead. Like most sports shows, the overall look was informal. We sat in canvas deck chairs, which at that time were considered very stylish.

One Saturday night as we were taping the show, I stretched back and accidentally caught the leg of my flimsy chair in the center crack of the stage. The next thing captured on tape was the bottom of my shoes as I fell over backwards. Nothing was hurt but my pride, and the tape kept rolling until I got up and cut to a commercial. Fred and I decided to broadcast the show in its entirety—complete with one of his players laughing so hard that he could hardly talk.

Separating Fred Taylor the man from Fred Taylor the coach is impossible. Like Woody Hayes, Fred was completely devoted to the game and to his players. Unlike Woody, his approach was basically low key. But both were extremely honest men and it was Fred's honesty that wound up "getting him resigned" from Ohio State.

I say "getting him resigned" because, although he wasn't fired, he was treated so poorly by the Big Ten and Ohio State's athletic director, Ed Weaver, that he felt he had no choice but to quit as head coach at the end of the 1975-76 season.

To get full retirement benefits, Fred stayed on to teach physical education and work with intramural sports until 1979. Then, with his 30 years in, he left the university to manage an exclusive country club near Columbus called The Golf Club. He's still there today and he's still, by anyone's standards, a class act.

Fred kept his public comments about the reason for his resignation to a minimum. He never engaged in mudslinging where Ed Weaver was concerned, but everyone knew his long-standing dislike of Weaver grew to feud proportions after the brawl at the Minnesota game in February 1972.

I remember it like it happened yesterday. At Williams Arena on the University of Minnesota campus with only thirty-six seconds left on the clock, Buckeye center Luke Witte scored on a jump shot. The Bucks were ahead 50-44 and naturally there was a lot of excitement in the arena. Things turned nasty seconds later when a Gopher forward named Corky Taylor walked up to Witte and decked him. When Witte started to get up, Corky Taylor slammed him in the groin with his knee and knocked him unconscious.

Then Minnesota player Ron Behagen ran over and began jumping on Witte's neck. That set off his teammates, who ran around like crazed animals attacking Buckeye players. One Gopher held down an Ohio State player while Minnesota fans beat him up. The brawling seemed to go on forever.

From my television booth I could spot only one police officer on the floor. Fred Taylor and Minnesota coach Bill Musselman were both down there trying to break it up.

Of course, there was no way the game could continue. Ohio State was declared the winner as Luke Witte, Mark Minor, and another Buckeye, Mark Wagar, all in serious condition, were carried off in an ambulance to the nearest hospital.

Meantime, Fred got the rest of the Ohio State team off the court and holed up with them in the locker room. The team feared for their lives, and rightly so. I was down there with them, and we waited for an hour and a half after the game before leaving the building. Even though it was bitterly cold, we were afraid Minnesota fans, who were used to the severe weather, might still be lurking outside. Finally, we were taken out through a steam tunnel to our bus. The driver kept the headlights off, and we quietly boarded, then literally sneaked out under the cover of darkness.

In all my years covering sports, I have never seen anything so frightening as the senseless, brutal violence I witnessed that night at Williams Arena. Musselman, who had a reputation for encouraging roughness, deserves a lot of the blame for his team's outrageous conduct. He is reputed to have had a sign in his locker room to the effect that "losing is worse than death." What kind of message does that give players?

John Gilligan, who was Ohio's governor at the time, called the Minnesota brawl the worst incident he'd ever seen in sports. You'd have expected Minnesota would have been thrown out for the season and fined. You'd have thought Musselman would have been fired. Instead, ringleaders Corky Taylor and Ron Behagen were suspended by a Big Ten commissioner for the rest of the season. That's it! Nothing else happened then or later to Musselman or his team, and Minnesota went on to win the Big Ten title that year.

Of course, Fred Taylor was devastated. He was shocked and bitter. Minnesota's athletic director had promised Weaver that strong action would be taken and, on the basis of this promise, Fred had advised Mark Wagar, who'd been badly injured, not to file a lawsuit.

However, Weaver didn't push for a stiffer penalty, and Fred spoke for many people when he told a sports reporter that the team had been left "high and dry." He added, "The Athletic Department's feeling was to bury the hatchet, while we got the hatchet buried in our heads."

To make matters worse, the team's performance deteriorated and the season ended poorly. Luke Witte even got booed by fans. It was as though in some twisted way, the Buckeyes had become the bad guys. And Weaver, dissatisfied with the team's performance, offered no support. The team's spirit was absolutely broken. I think Fred's was too, because Ohio State's performance steadily declined. Before the Minnesota game, the Buckeyes had a .750 winning percentage. Afterwards, it fell to .460. During Fred's last three years as coach, the Buckeyes were 9-15, 14-14 and 6-20.

I'm not claiming that the Minnesota incident was directly responsible for everything that happened in the following seasons, but Weaver's lack of support was certainly a major factor. Fred knew Ohio State's recruiting efforts weren't as strong as they should have been, and he was criticized because many good high school players had gone to out-of-state colleges. To remedy the situation, he developed a plan that entailed hiring some assistants to help with recruiting. Weaver shot it down.

It's not that Fred Taylor didn't want to recruit the best possible players. It's that he refused to play dirty to get them. Unlike some of his colleagues, Fred didn't go after players who couldn't meet Ohio State's admission requirements. Many of these players were black and, as a result, some people called him a racist, which was absolutely ridiculous.

My friend Kaye Kessler, sports writer for the old *Columbus Citizen Journal*, wrote at the time: "What Fred hasn't done with black athletes is take them if they didn't qualify. He's always shied away from hardship cases and non-predictors. He was criticized, for example, when two black players from Columbus East High School, Nick Connor and Ed Ratleff, went elsewhere. Well, it's a known fact that Connor's high school class ranking was changed so he could get into Illinois, and Ratleff went to Long Beach State but couldn't qualify at Ohio State."

In explaining why he stuck with his standards, Fred said publicly, "I didn't cheat for Jerry Lucas or John Havlicek so I'm certainly not going to cheat today. There's a lot of under-the-table stuff going on." To his credit, Fred Taylor wanted no part of it. Fred also deserves praise for the standards he maintained for the players on his teams. But, of course, many people didn't see it that way at the time.

During his last season as coach, Fred benched a player named Wardell Jackson because Jackson was hotdogging it with his eyes on pro recruiters in the stands, rather than giving his attention to the game. Supposedly, Jackson retaliated by spreading the word to potential black recruits that Fred Taylor was a racist. Larry Bolden, an outstanding black player on the 1976 team, disputed these accusations, telling reporters that Fred had been like a father to him.

Even Ohio State's student newspaper, *The Lantern*, which ordinarily loved to go after coaches, jumped to Fred's defense. In the winter of 1976, a student reporter named Mark Mills wrote, "He doesn't promise the moon to young, impressionable athletes, he doesn't try to see how he can bend recruiting laws and fix grades. Fred Taylor stands out as one of the greatest coaches in America. He is one of a dying breed."

To turn around an old expression, right doesn't make might, and all Fred's principles and coaching ability couldn't turn around a losing team. The Buckeyes finished last in the Big Ten that season. Following years of pressure from Ed Weaver, Fred Taylor quit.

Weaver had twice denied the man raises, and, even before the Minnesota fiasco, had taken away all but eight of Fred's previously generous allotment of complimentary football tickets. Even during Taylor's early years at Ohio State there had been harsh words and actions. The relationship between them deteriorated into something that fell between awful and—because they rarely spoke—nonexistent.

It wasn't surprising, therefore, that Fred chose to avoid Weaver and meet with Harold Enarson, then Ohio State's president, to tender his resignation in February 1976. Enarson, who three years later hardly batted an eye when he fired Woody Hayes after the Gator Bowl incident, reluctantly accepted Fred's resignation with deep regret. He set up a Fred R. Taylor Scholarship Fund with a $10,000 permanent endowment and asked Fred to specify the criteria for selecting the recipient. In a formal letter accepting the resignation, Enarson praised Fred's many achievements, and shared a conversation he'd had with a member of the search committee that brought Fred to Ohio State.

"Recently I happened to talk to a leader in the community who had served on the Search Committee which recommended you for the job, [Enarson wrote.] *He said something like this: 'We were looking for someone who understood that a player is a student first and foremost, that excellence and good sportsmanship must go hand-in-hand, and that a good coach is a friend, confidant, and above all, a teacher. In watching Fred for eighteen years, I felt that in every way he lived up to our highest expectations.'"* President Enarson added his own words: "Everyone who has watched you will agree."

Fred's overall record is a testament to President Enarson's comments. During his tenure, Ohio State basketball teams won 297 of the 455 games they played, for a winning percentage of .654. Under Fred Taylor, the Buckeyes lost only four of 18 NCAA tournament games and won seven Big Ten championships—five of the seven were in successive seasons, setting an all-time Big Ten record. Among his other records: 32 straight victories, 50 straight wins at home and 27 straight Big Ten victories.

In 1986, Fred Taylor received the recognition that has always been his due when he was inducted into the Basketball Hall of Fame. One of the few Ohio State players or coaches to receive this honor—John Havlicek is also a Hall of Famer—Fred was naturally overjoyed with the news, but he responded in his typical modest way.

"I don't want you to think I'm on an ego trip," he told a reporter, "but it's pretty exciting to think that someone thought enough of me to make me an honoree. I'd be lying if I didn't say I was tickled to death about this."

And so were all the rest of us. How about that, sports fans!

5

Coaches Eldon, Gary and Randy

When Eldon Miller came to Ohio State as head basketball coach in 1976, he arrived with a great season of 25 wins, 3 losses behind him at Western Michigan. With good cause, he radiated the gentlemanly confidence and quiet optimism that had always marked his style.

And, like anyone who makes the step up to a premier Big Ten school, Eldon was thrilled to be at Ohio State. "It's unbelievable," he told *Columbus Dispatch* reporter Paul Hornung, who interviewed him on his first day as OSU's head basketball coach. "I've been an Ohio State fan ever since I was old enough to pick up a ball."

In the end, Ohio State was not a fan of Eldon Miller. When he learned ten years later that he was out of a job, Eldon told a caller on his WBNS radio show who'd asked about his future plans: "I have no idea. It might be coaching basketball. It might be selling Wendy's Frosties. It's hard to tell."

As everyone knows, Eldon did not wind up selling milk shakes. Three weeks later, Northern Iowa gave him a five-year contract as head basketball coach—something Ohio State, which refused to make a multi-year agreement, never did.

I've shared my opinions about Eldon's career at Ohio State in chapter six, so I'll be brief in this one. Eldon was fired on February 3, 1986, and the incident was on Woody Hayes' mind February 14th when thirty or so of his friends gathered at Ohio State's ROTC building to celebrate Woody's seventy-first birthday. He lived to celebrate only one more birthday, and the knowledge that time was running out made Woody more honest and outspoken than ever.

After we'd cut the cake and sung "Happy Birthday," Woody went around the room and thanked each of us personally for coming. When he got to me, he said, "I respect this guy for all he's done for children—even if he didn't get along with our basketball coach." Woody was referring to my WCMH commentary that had aired shortly before Eldon was fired—or quit, if you believe former OSU Athletic Director Rick Bay—on why I thought it was time for Ohio State to find a new head basketball coach.

Later, I took Woody aside and explained the reasoning behind my statement: Eldon had been able to recruit only two of the past ten Class AAA players of the year, and high school basketball coaches weren't recommending OSU to their top athletes. My remarks came on the heels of a 87-75 loss to Minnesota—the fifth loss in six games.

Woody listened patiently to my explanation, then cocked his head and said, "You're right. We didn't play too well up at Minnesota, did we? If we'd had somebody up there [like Indiana coach Bobby Knight] to throw a chair across the floor, we might have won the goddam ball game!"

That was standard Woody humor and, of course, he wasn't serious. Like nearly everyone else, Woody liked and respected Eldon Miller. During his years at Ohio State, Eldon had some wonderful successes. In ten years, he took the Buckeyes to six post-season tournaments.

In 1982 and again in 1983, United Press International voted him Big Ten Coach of the Year. The 1982 award followed a 1981 record of 14 wins and 13 losses. In typically modest style, he told a reporter after the 1982 award, "I think it's very important, when you've had a bad year, to come back with a good one. We've been able to do that."

Unfortunately, due to poor recruiting, Eldon wasn't able to consistently wind up with good years. His teams won 98 and lost 86 in Big Ten play.

Indiana University coach Bob Knight, who stormed out of a secret interview for Miller's old job, praised Eldon's integrity. "In all the years I've known Eldon, I've never questioned his honesty in regard to the way he runs his program," Knight told a reporter the day after Miller was fired. "There are an awful lot of guys you can't say that about."

Eldon took full responsibility for the Buckeyes' recruiting problems and poor record. The man exhibited incredible grace under pressure. Unlike some other OSU coaches, Eldon didn't whine or place the blame on his players. Two days after it was announced that his contract would not be renewed, Eldon told a reporter, "He [OSU Athletic Director Rick Bay] fired me, and I accepted the fact that he fired me. . . . We came here to win basketball games and we didn't win enough. That's the bottom line: winning. . . . Is someone to blame? Sure. I am."

Ohio State moved quickly to replace Eldon with Boston College coach Gary Williams, who was hired on March 15, 1986, and given a five-year contract. Eldon, meanwhile, stayed on until June to finish out his one-year contract.

Williams was as high-key as Miller was low-key. Ohio State's tenth head basketball coach sweated and stomped and yelled and waved his arms. Gary Williams gave it his all, and man did it show! *Dispatch* reporter Mike Sullivan described Williams to a T when he wrote: "When Williams leaves the St. John Arena court at halftime, shoulders rolling as he walks behind his team, you expect that at any moment he will bounce into the air, fly straight over the players' heads, and crash through the door of the locker room."

In short order, the sheer force of his personality combined with his upbeat coaching style put the enthusiasm back into Ohio State basketball. Another smart thing Williams did that got people fired up about OSU basketball was to seat students back down close to the floor in the area that had long been reserved for the big alumni donors. Unlike the alums, the students were undignified and loud—and I believe their yelling and screaming did more to directly spur the team on than any financial contributions could have done.

The fans had big expectations for Williams, and so did the university. His was the first multi-year contract ever awarded a basketball coach in Ohio State's history. Although he wasn't the university's first choice—Virginia's Terry Holland and Jim Boeheim of Syracuse, Mike Krzyzewski of Duke, and Tennessee's Don DeVoe were all mentioned for the job—people looked to Williams to turn the Buckeyes around. He didn't let them down. By the time the Bucks beat Western Michigan in the second game of Williams' first season, fans were chanting "Ga-ree, Ga-ree," as he headed for the locker room.

Gary rode his players hard and more than one observer remarked that he and Woody Hayes shared a similar explosive temperament. At the end of practice sessions that hadn't gone well, he was heard to roar that nobody was leaving until the team decided they weren't going to be mediocre players. For the most part, players did not take his comments personally, and they flourished under his leadership.

Treg Lee, an All-American from Cleveland, said Williams' intensity was what made him choose Ohio State. Dennis Hopson, a Toledo native who was one of Williams' top forwards, said players eventually learned to see Williams' temper as motivational. "It was kind of scary at first," he told a reporter. "But I realize now that coach needs that emotion to get us going."

Leading scorer Jay Burson said, "Minute-to-minute, you don't know if he's going to jump on you. I've taken it personally at times but I have to realize he's trying to make me a better player."

Clearly, getting guys to perform to their maximum was his number-one goal, and if that required screaming and intimidation, so be it. Williams often said that he never wanted to see his players outhustled, and he was a master at firing them up to do their best.

Some highlights: In December, 1986, the Buckeyes upset Kansas 79-78 in overtime and Florida 88-84 in the Rainbow Classic in Honolulu. In March 1987, Ohio State beat the University of Kentucky 91-77 in first-round play of the NCAA Tournament. In 1989, Ohio State beat third-ranked Louisville 85-79.

There were plenty of well-deserved complimentary broadcasts and articles about Williams during his three years at Ohio State. There were also plenty of rumors that he was considering other offers.

In March of his second year at Ohio State, he said that despite being mentioned as a candidate for the job by a Providence newspaper, he was not considering the head coach job at Providence College. A month later, he denied interest in being the head coach of an NBA expansion team, the Charlotte Hornets, even though he met in North Carolina with team officials. In June, 1988, he removed his name from consideration for the head basketball coach's job at the University of Kansas.

In each instance, Williams emphasized that he was happy at Ohio State. "My goals at Ohio State haven't been met yet," he told a reporter. "I don't consider myself justified in considering another job because of my commitment here . . . If you were in my position, where would you want to go?"

A year later Gary Williams had an answer to that question—back to the University of Maryland, his alma mater. When word leaked out in June 1989 that he'd been offered the job, Ohio State offered a three-year extension to his five-year contract, which still had two years to run. Columbus businessmen put together two different annuities to try to keep him at Ohio State.

In accepting the Maryland job, Williams said money and job security were not issues. At Ohio State, he earned a base salary of about $83,000. Product endorsements, radio and TV shows, and other outside income brought the figure to a whopping $500,000. At Maryland, his base salary was $125,000 with $75,000 guaranteed from radio and TV shows.

"People who've accused me of taking the Maryland job for money are sadly mistaken," he stated. "I really thought Ohio State would be the job for me," he added. "They did everything they could for me, and I appreciate that. I guess the Maryland job has always been in the back of my mind."

Gary Williams had always been a hotly pursued coach. The year before he left Boston College he received offers from Arkansas and Wake Forest, which he refused. The following year, he wisely jumped at Ohio State's offer and I give him a lot of credit for infusing new life into the Bucks' basketball program. If Gary had been upfront all along about his desire to eventually return to Maryland, I would have wished him godspeed and good luck. Instead, I think he used Ohio State as a stepping stone.

The fact that the Buckeyes' leading scorer Jay Burson retired due to a shoulder injury—causing the team to lose eight of its final ten games— must also have affected Williams' decision to leave. But by not honoring his five-year contract, he let down Toledo Macomber's Jim Jackson and the other fine athletes who came to Ohio State specifically to play under the direction of Gary Williams.

On his way out of town, Williams recommended Randy Ayers—who he also asked to join him at Maryland as an assistant coach—as his successor.

Randy had been hired in 1983 as an assistant to Eldon Miller and had been asked by Gary to stay on in 1986 when Williams took over.

Instead of promptly following Williams' excellent suggestion, the university conducted a national search for a head basketball coach. They looked at thirty potential candidates, one of the hottest being Nolan Richardson of Arkansas. Two days after Richardson withdrew from consideration, the university on July 3, 1989, named Randy Ayers Ohio State's eleventh head basketball coach and awarded him a five-year contract.

I don't think the university could have made a better selection than Randy, but they didn't handle the process very well. It looked like the six-member search committee offered him the job by default. I don't believe that was their reasoning—but I do believe their PR was clumsy in the way they went about selecting Randy Ayers for the job.

Randy certainly had his work cut out for him. He inherited a team with no seniors. Only three players had ever been starters. Center Perry Carter would miss a month of preseason practice due to a bruised kidney that kept him sidelined. And Treg Lee had been been hit with a one-game suspension because of his unauthorized competition in a basketball tournament during summer vacation.

Randy Ayers was more than equal to the task. Although he had no previous head coaching experience, Ayers had solid experience has an assistant coach at West Point and under his predecessors, Eldon Miller and Gary Williams.

He'd had solid playing experience as well. During his senior year at North High School in Springfield, he had been named Class AAA player of the year. In college, the 6'6" Ayers started for four years as a forward for the Miami University Redskins, and served as team captain his senior year. After college, he tried out for the Chicago Bulls but didn't make the final cut.

At the tender age of 33, Randy Ayers knew basketball inside and out. Another plus was that he also knew the Ohio State players inside and out. In fact, he had recruited many of them and had often smoothed over their bruised egos following tongue-lashings by Gary Williams.

Several of the players told me they wanted Randy as their head coach. They also told OSU Athletic Director Jim Jones, who said the players' support of Ayers played a role in his selection. Guard Jamaal Brown's comments when he learned Randy Ayers had been promoted to head coach were illustrative of the way the team felt about Ayers. "This is what most of the players wanted," he told a reporter. "We won't skip a beat. It's not like having a new coach come in."

The move from assistant to head coach was, Ayers admitted, a major jump. At the end of his first season, he put it this way: "Someone once said those 18 inches along the bench [that separate an assistant coach from the head coach] are the biggest move you'll ever make, and it's true."

Being the youngest coach in the Big Ten and the only black coach probably also put him under extra scrutiny. Still, at a press conference three months into the job, when he assured us he was having a ball, it was obvious that he was telling the truth.

Randy's first season was a tough one. The Buckeyes won 17 and lost 13, but showed steady improvement. They won nine of their last 13 games and advanced to the second round of the NCAA Tournament. As the players' performances improved, so did their grades. During Ayers first year, the team's grade point average was higher than it had been in a dozen years.

As everyone knows, in his second year Ayers led the Buckeyes to a 15-3 league record and Ohio State's first Big Ten title in twenty years. It's little wonder that Randy Ayers—the second-youngest coach ever to receive the award—was named the 1991 Big Ten Coach of the Year. (Bobby Knight was 32 when he first received the award in 1973). Ayers was also named National Coach of the Year by the AP, the Basketball Writers Association, the Black Coaches Association of America and *Basketball Weekly.*

He was pleased, of course, but in the spring of 1991 was not resting on his laurels. "The thing is," he said, looking to the future, "we've got to sustain this."

They did—with an overall record of 21 wins, 5 losses during the 1991/92 season and 13-3 in the Big Ten, winning the Big Ten championship for the second year in a row, thanks to outstanding playing as well as fine coaching.

Jim Jackson recovered from the stress injury that put his left foot and leg in a cast during the Pan-Am Games the previous summer and had a fantastic season, raising his average point-per-game score to 24. During Ohio State's four NCAA Tournament games he scored a total of 74 points.

Lawrence Funderburke mellowed out of his reputation as a "dirty player" and also had a great season. How many people still make a big deal about the fact that Funderburke quit IU and walked out on Bob Knight on Christmas Eve 1989? By the time OSU got knocked out of the NCAA Southeast Regional final by Michigan (75-71 in overtime), Funderburke had totaled 63 points in Ohio State's four tournament games.

Bill Robinson, at 7 feet and 255 pounds of solid muscle, also showed a lot of might that season. Senior guard Jamaal Brown had a fantastic season, too. He became the thirty-second player in Buckeye history to score 1,000 points during his career. Chris Jent, Mark Baker, and their other teammates also performed well.

Under Randy Ayers' fine leadership, the Buckeyes played their hearts out in the NCAA Tournament. When the team arrived back in Columbus after the heart-breaking Michigan loss, they were welcomed by hordes of fans at St. John Arena.

Always the gentleman, Ayers managed to set aside his personal feelings of disappointment about being knocked out of the tournament, and was able to put the whole thing in perspective. "In a couple of days," he told the crowd, "we're going to reflect back on this experience with a lot of satisfaction."

I think the team's less than stellar performance during the 1992-93 season was what everyone expected. Before the season started, I predicted Ohio State would finish fifth or sixth, right in the middle of the pack. As it turned out, they finished seventh in the Big Ten.

I don't think Randy Ayers should be criticized. When you lose a Chris Jent, a Jamaal Brown and a Mark Baker—all of whom graduated in 1992—and a Jimmy Jackson, who signed with the pros, you can't expect anything to follow but a rebuilding year. Last season, the team had only two seniors, Tom Brandewie and Alex Davis, and a lot of freshman. Woody Hayes used to say, "The best thing about freshmen is that someday they become sophomores." I'm sure Randy Ayers would agree.

Still, during the course of the season, Ohio State defeated the number one team in the nation, Indiana, in overtime. They came up against Michigan, ranked third, a couple of weeks later and lost by only two points. The team showed it has talent. Now it's just going to take some time to develop it. I look for Ohio State, with Randy Ayers at the helm, to be a dominant power in basketball for years to come.

6

Why Did I Say That?

For years, I've received letters and calls from sports fans telling me to keep my opinions to myself. I've gotten much more feedback, however, applauding my outspoken ways. In most instances, the positive responses have outnumbered the negative ones by at least ten to one. But even if the numbers were reversed, I'd still feel an obligation to speak my piece. I'm proud to say that WCMH-TV has always supported and encouraged this position.

I've spent the last fifty years observing and reporting on sports and I think I've learned a little bit along the way. Because of my first-hand access to people and events, it's no surprise that I've developed some insight into how things in the sports world should work. When they don't work the way they should—say, when a coach loses his effectiveness but not his job, or when an effective coach is canned—I feel obligated to speak out.

The kinds of situations I've spoken out about go beyond the individuals involved. They are ethical issues that affect the lives of many people— coaches, fans, players and potential recruits. My comments have never been based on my personal feelings.

If I let my heart dictate my head, I'd never criticize anyone. My mother always said, "Jimmy, if you can't say something nice, don't say anything at all," and when it comes to personal relationships, that's been my rule of thumb. Professionally, however, I can't let those feelings stand in the way of honest criticism.

I thought the world of Woody Hayes, but I didn't hesitate to criticize his temper tantrums. Former Buckeye basketball coach Eldon Miller is a personal friend. One reason we know each other so well is because I hosted "The Eldon Miller Show" from 1984 to 1986 on WCMH-TV. Yet, when his performance began to affect recruiting, I felt it was my duty to say so. When Earle Bruce, who was a damned good coach, was fired by Ed Jennings, then president of OSU, to appease wealthy alumni, I spoke for a lot of angry fans when I blasted Jennings' actions on the air. Public opinion was on my side, and I have a box full of letters from fans to prove it.

Of course, my opinions haven't always been popular. My condemnation of Woody's behavior during a 1971 game against Michigan made a lot of fans furious. Angry over a bad call, Woody had gone into a rage and broken sideline markers over his knees, torn the trappings from chains around the field and just generally lost control. The following day, as I entered the press box at Riverfront Stadium in Cinncinati to broadcast the Bengals' game, I was bombarded with questions from reporters asking not about OSU's loss against Michigan, but about Woody's behavior at Ann Arbor.

There were no questions about the Buckeyes' magnificent defense, no comments about Tom Campana's brilliant punt returns. Instead, reporters talked only about Woody's temper tantrum—a tantrum that took the focus off football and put it on an episode that caused the university great embarrassment. That's basically what I later said on the air. I expected to receive some criticism from diehard fans who believed Woody could do no wrong, and that's exactly what I got.

For all their righteous anger, though, some of the letters were hilarious. I still get a chuckle out of them more than twenty years later. Here's an excerpt from my favorite. It's from an Ohio veterinarian who also happened to be a rabid Buckeye fan.

"You have been my favorite sportscaster, but last Tuesday I was

completely shocked by your outburst on Coach Hayes. I thought your eyes were going to pop out as you read your little gem. [Note: I've been told my eyes always look like they're going to pop out.] *It was rotten, Jimmy, simply rotten. . . . You owe Coach Hayes an apology, as well as millions of Buckeye fans. I for one can never think highly of you again until I hear this apology. Jimmy, it was crummy and Tuesday night you were an awfully little crumb."*

The veterinarian wasn't the first sports fan to tell me off, and he probably won't be the last. I can usually handle criticism cheerfully. I would not have been able to last if this business if I hadn't developed a tough professional hide. I've learned, though, that even contrary sports fans deserve a courteous response. Here's a bit of what I wrote back:

"Even though you disagree with my criticism of Woody Hayes for his actions during the recent Ohio State-Michigan game, you and I apparently have one thing in common—we both have great respect and admiration for Woody as a coach . . . Woody has often said he is not here to win a popularity poll, and he pulls no punches when he takes a verbal slap at something or someone . . . In this respect, I think we all have to remember that it is a two-way street."

I also sent a copy of my letter to Woody. If he was mad at me, I never heard about it. Apparently he didn't think I was out of line for publicly expressing my opinion.

The controversy that got stirred up over my comments about former OSU basketball coach Eldon Miller was not about his behavior. At Ohio State, Eldon always acted like a gentleman. Instead, I was concerned about Eldon's inability to recruit good Ohio high school stars for the Buckeyes. I decided it was time to speak up when the Bucks lost on January 30, 1986, to the Minnesota Gophers, whose best players had been disqualified because of various infractions.

Before I went on the air, I talked with WCMH news anchor Doug Adair about the best way to phrase my comment. I decided to be simple and direct, saying only, "I think it's time for OSU Athletic Director Rick Bay to begin looking for a new basketball coach," before moving into my report on the game. My public comment brought into the open what many people had been saying privately for quite some time.

During his ten years at Ohio State, Eldon recruited only two of the past ten Class AAA players-of-the-year: Herb Williams and Clark Kellogg. Over the years, he'd lost Gary Grant to Michigan, Jerome Ladd to Pittsburgh, Grady Mateen to Georgetown, and Todd Mitchell to Purdue, to name just a few who got away.

Because of the Buckeyes' fine reputation, Eldon did fairly well in recruiting his first couple of seasons. When he left Western Michigan to take the Ohio State job in 1976-77 season, he brought Jim Ellinghausen with him and signed superstar Kelvin Ransey, who became Ohio State's twelfth All-America player. He also recruited Herb Williams from Columbus' Marion-Franklin High School.

Williams was joined by two other Columbus players: Marquis Miller of St. Charles and Todd Penn of Linden McKinley High School. Barberton, Ohio, star Carter Scott and Cleveland East Tech star Jim Smith completed his roster of Ohio players. To top it off, Eldon also recruited Kenny Page, an All-American from New York.

Despite the quality of his teams, Eldon's record the first two years was 11 wins, 16 losses in the 1977, flipping to 16 wins, 11 losses in 1978. It wasn't until 1980 that the team got it all together and gave Eldon his best record of 21-8. The record didn't help, though, when the team lost to UCLA 72-68 in the NCAA West Regional Final.

Most fans thought Ohio State should have won—especially since Ransey, Williams and Kellogg went on to play in the NBA. Fans were really griping by the end of 1981 season when, with Kellogg, Smith, Williams, Penn and Scott still on the team, half the games were lost.

Ohio high school coaches were griping, too, and their gripes are even more important than those of the fans. Their top high school players naturally want to go to the university that has the most successful basketball program. These players turn to their high school coaches for advice when selecting universities. I felt high school coaches were already down on Eldon at that point. I know they were by 1984, because I was told so by an old friend who's a high school coach. At the time, he was an official with the Ohio High School Basketball Coaches Association.

I'd heard of a standout player at his school and called to ask him where the kid would be going to college. He told me, "I'm not sure yet, but it's not going to be Ohio State. I've told him he'll jeopardize his career if he goes to OSU because the program and the coaching are so bad." He added, "Jim, I can tell you that I know from my position in the Basketball Association that other coaches feel the same way. They're all steering their kids away from Ohio State."

This man, like nearly everyone else I know, had no axes to grind with Eldon as a person. He was simply advising his players to do what he felt was best for them. Unfortunately, what was best for them was not what was best for Ohio State. His comments about Eldon's coaching and recruiting record were typical of remarks I had been hearing everywhere—remarks I'm sure Eldon was aware of.

Like any other fan, I want to see kids raised in Ohio stay in Ohio. I don't like to see them go to out-of-state schools and then come back to kick Ohio State's butt. My feeling was that expecting Eldon to do a good job without the support of the high school coaches was like expecting miracles from a major league team that lacks minor league support. In order to get top college players, coaches must rely on the high schools that are, in effect, farm teams. If he can't attract these players, a college coach is sunk.

Ohio State Athletic Director Jim Jones told me shortly after I had publicly commented that OSU needed a new coach that he had talked with Eldon five years before about stepping down. "I told him I thought he'd gone as far as he could with the basketball program at Ohio State," Jim told me.

At the time, Jim Jones was an assistant director with no authority to hire and fire coaches. His advice to Eldon was motivated solely by friendship. Obviously, Eldon didn't listen. Things got so bad that by the 1985-86 season—his last—Eldon was booed at some of the home games.

After Eldon was fired on February 3, 1986, the team's performance picked up and they went on to win the National Invitational Tournament in Madison Square Garden. Since even the players who criticized his coaching liked Eldon personally, this may have been a case of "winning one for the Gipper." Eldon's comment to reporters after one of the NIT games was typical of his generosity of spirit. Zan Hale, sports reporter for the *Columbus Dispatch*, called the March 26 win "a swan song for a lame duck." Eldon's comment was more positive. "I live in the magic of the moment," he told reporters. "I don't live in the past. I don't live too far in the future. I have to find another magic moment."

Actually, he'd already found one. A little more than three weeks after he was fired—or resigned—depending on who's talking, Eldon accepted a five-year contract as head coach at the University of Northern Iowa in Cedar Falls. He left Ohio State with a record of 94 wins, 81 losses.

Even after Eldon had happily signed with Northern Iowa, I was still getting hate mail from fans. Here's an excerpt from one I received on March 4th—one month after my comment and a week after Eldon had taken the job with Iowa for the 1986-87 season.

"Dear Coach Crumb,

As I recall, some years ago you were hit in the head with a hockey puck at the Coliseum, and the headline in the Citizen Journal read, 'X-rays of Crum's head reveal nothing.' Today, more than ever, that headline is valid."

The letter went on to criticize my "hatchet job" on Eldon and urged me to "unhook my navel from my backbone" and "help the next coach instead of tearing him down."

That one really did hurt, although I still can't figure out what he meant by my navel being hooked to my backbone. It certainly wasn't a reference to the size of my waist. My comments about Eldon were made with the best interests of the Ohio State basketball program in mind. My simple statement—"I think it's time OSU Athletic Director Rick Bay began looking for another basketball coach"—sparked a lot of debate and, indirectly, resulted in a much-needed and long-overdue change at the university.

One thing I've learned about voicing strong opinions is that if you remain true to yourself and continue to speak up, the public is bound to jump back in your corner eventually. That's exactly what happened a year and a half later in November of 1987 when I criticized Ed Jennings, then president of Ohio State, for the firing of Earle Bruce.

Columbus Monthly called it "the week the town went crazy," and I certainly can't improve on that. Most people are familiar with the facts: Two days after a 29-27 loss to Iowa in Ohio Stadium on November 14, 1987, Ohio State president Ed Jennings forced OSU athletic director Rick Bay to fire head football coach Earle Bruce.

The loss to Iowa was Ohio State's third straight Big Ten loss, and fans were, to say the least, disturbed. The Buckeyes had been leading 27-22 prior to the last thirty seconds of the game. Still, few people—probably least of all, Earle Bruce—expected his firing. According to Rick Bay, it came as a complete surprise.

After axing Earle, Bay—who's since bounced around at a number of jobs—resigned in protest. Bruce didn't take it lying down, either. He filed a $7.4 million lawsuit against Ed Jennings and Ohio State for breach of the three-year contract he signed in June of 1986. Earle and his attorney, the late John Zonak, requested a jury trial but later settled out of court.

Earle never achieved the "grand old man" status of Woody Hayes at Ohio State. He just didn't have Woody's kind of charisma, but then neither did anyone else. People poked fun at Earle's weight. They made fun of the way he dressed. There was also some complaining about his alleged gambling. Some said he was greedy because he station-hopped to get the biggest possible bucks for his football show.

But no one can dispute this fact: With an 81-26-1 record, Earle was the "winningest coach in the Big Ten." That and only that is what he should have been judged on. It was widely felt that firing him after the loss to Iowa (and before the win over Michigan) made Ohio State look like a football factory. Ironically, this was an image former OSU President Ed Jennings had worked hard to change.

Why Jennings didn't anticipate the furor that would occur and the horrible light in which the firing put the university is beyond me. I honestly think the man was astonished by the public outcry, and stunned when angry alumni cancelled thousands of dollars in pledges to Ohio State's Development Fund. Not only did he make Ohio State look bad, but Jennings—who was going through a divorce—had his own name dragged through the mud as tongues wagged about his personal life.

Here's what I said about Jennings' actions in my sports commentary:

"Since I began covering Ohio State in 1951, I have always had great respect for the university, the administration, and especially for those who are charged with the responsibility of running a first-class operation—people like [former OSU presidents] Dr. Bevis and Dr. Fawcett.

"It's too bad we don't have someone like these men in charge of the university now. Because of the way this was handled—because of the crushing blow that has been dealt to a couple of class guys like Earle Bruce and and Rick Bay—I have lost all respect for Ohio State's president.

"Less than a week ago, the university president was saying, 'Now's the time to support Earle Bruce and the Buckeyes. Now's the time to show them we care.' Today—apparently because of pressure brought to bear by wealthy alums who threatened to withhold financial support unless Earle Bruce was replaced—that president forgot all about what was right and what was wrong.

"He chose to forget that Earle was the winningest coach in the Big ten during the past nine years; that he'd won more than seventy-five percent of his games. The bottom line in his decision-making process had nothing to do with athletic or academic achievements. The well-being of the coach, the athletic director and the student athletes had nothing to do with it. The bottom line was money—and that, my friends, is wrong."

That commentary won me an award for reporting from the Cleveland Press Club. Ohio State fans were also overwhelmingly in my corner. Both before and after my commentary, the calls and letters received by the station ran strongly against Jennings. Ninety percent of the more than 12,000 viewers who called the station to vote in our phone poll disapproved of the way Earl Bruce was fired. Here's a sampling of what angry fans had to say in the hundred or so letters I received:

From a fan who signed himself "ashamed to be a Buckeye": *"Don't let it die! Members of the Board of Trustees who refuse to listen to the majority can be replaced along with Jennings! This whole situation stinks!"*

From an alum in Virginia who sent along a petition requesting that Earle Bruce be reinstated as head football coach: *"What is really irritating to me is the fact that a few high-dollar contributing alumni have forced their wishes on the rest of the Ohio State supporters. If I had written a letter to Jennings wanting Earle fired, I'm sure it would have found its way into file thirteen."*

From a local minister: *"Thank you for your editorial regarding the massacre of coach Earle Bruce. You spoke clearly and forthrightly. Certainly, the confidence any of us had in the administration of Dr. Edward Jennings was badly shaken! Thank you for articulating our feelings."*

My favorite is from a fan who signed herself simply, "a lady from Lancaster." Here's what she said: *"Hi Ya, Mr. J.C.—I admire you for coming on TV and telling it like it is. It's a rotten dirty trick. Poor Earle. Jennings should resign or be fired. He acts like he's from outer space!"*

As the world knows, all the public outcry amounted to naught. Shortly after filing the suit, Earle's attorney settled out of court with the university's attorney, John Elam. Earle received a lump-sum payment of $471,000, with the provision that he'd return part of it if he took another coaching job before July 1, 1989, when his contract with Ohio State expired.

In June, 1988, Earle signed a four-year contract with the University of Northern Iowa—the same school that had scooped up Eldon Miller after his firing by Ohio State. After only a year at Northern Iowa, Earle left to take a job as head coach at Colorado State, which fired him in the fall of 1992 after he admitted committing NCAA violations and punching players.

Earle was also accused of making racist comments. He denied this charge, and I believe he was being truthful. Earle had a fine relationship with African American players at Ohio State.

Earle's firing came as a major shock to me. I never knew Earle to violate any rules—he always had a good, clean record. That's why it amazed me that he knowingly violated NCAA rules about giving his players a day off practice each week. Glenn Mason, head coach at Kansas, told me Earle had called him last season and asked if he gave his players the required day off. Glenn said yes, and that's when Earle told him that he was working his kids seven days a week. He certainly should have known better.

As to the charge of punching his players—any guy who's every played football has had his coach pound him on the arm or shoulder! Woody Hayes even gave his kids occasional kicks in the rear. Football practice is like Marine boot camp, which is why I hate hearing crybabies come up with that "He hit me" stuff.

Earle owned up to his mistakes, saying "I take full responsibility for them." He settled out of court with the university for about $100,000 on the remaining years of his contract.

I played golf with Earle in June, 1993, at Winding Hollow Country Club for the NetCare Tournament, a charity fundraiser that Earle has been honorary chairman of since he was at Ohio State. He told me he and his wife have built a house in Wilmington, North Carolina—which, by the way, is the home of Chicago Bulls superstar Michael Jordan. Earle has relatives in Wilmington, which is one reason he's decided to move there.

Earle told me he loved Colorado and said he'd like to stay in coaching and would listen to any offers that might come along. Coaching is Earle's life, and he misses it. He's philosophical about the chance of that happening, though, and told me, "Jimmy, if it's not meant to be, it's not meant to be."

In August, Earle got back into the game in another way when he was hired by WTVN Radio to do pre- and post-game analysis for the 1993 Ohio State football season. He will also make appearances on WTVN's "Bucks Line," and any other programs having to do with Ohio State football. He has rented a condo in Columbus and will be here from September through December for the football season.

There have not been any hard feelings between Earle and me, and I'm overjoyed that he's working for WTVN. It's been the Athletic Department at Ohio State that holds grudges. Jack Schrom, a packager who put together the first season of Randy Ayers' television show, told me later that he had pencilled me in as the show's host.

Schrom said the university told him "No way! Crum has criticized our president and criticized our athletic program and there's no way we're going to allow him to be host of the Randy Ayers Show!"

So my straightforwardness cost me a job, I guess, and some money. But I really didn't care. I'm here to do a job and it wasn't the first time I had spoken mind. And, as anyone knows who heard my commentaries on John Cooper, it wasn't my last.

I had more hair in 1929 at age 1, than I do at 65 in 1993.

Here I am posing at age 11 with the apple of my eye, my six-month-old sister, Judy.

My wedding day, April 18, 1954. Congratulating Miriam and me are my grandparents, Margaret and James Crum.

PFC James W. Crum, serial number 626522, served in the U.S. Marine Corps from 1946-1948.

This was our set at Channel 4 for the 13-week "Big Bear Hunt" series in 1956. With me are the two bears that Dick von Maur and I shot on Alaska's Kodiak Island.

A year after the trip to Kodiak Island, we got our own little cub, Kelly Jean Crum. She was more afraid of the camera than she was of the bear skin rug.

I described my adventures as a "big bear hunter" on Kodiak Island in 1956 to Sally Flowers, and Billy Scott, co-star of the long running Columbus TV show, "Meeting' Time at Moore's."

At Louis Bromfield's Malabar Farm south of Mansfield, Judge Herb Shettler chatted with Lauren Bacall and Humphrey Bogart after performing their wedding ceremony. Harold Robinson and I covered the event for WMAN, Mansfield.

I interviewed one of the all-time great boxers, former middleweight champion Sugar Ray Robinson. Note the call letters on the microphone and my mop of dark hair.

I chatted with former Cleveland Indians pitcher and baseball Hall of Famer Bob Feller on one of our first studio sets, back when WCMH was still known as WLW-C Channel 3.

In 1963, my son Jimmy–2-feet 9 inches and 30 lbs.–gave some pointers to OSU Buckeye guard Doug Van Horne, who carried 226 lbs. on his 6-foot 2-inch frame.

I got a boost from "Meetin' Time at Moore's" co-star Billy Scott when I interviewed former heavyweight boxer Primo Carnera, who lost to Joe Louis.

I talked to Buckeye football stars Bobby Watkins, Dick Brubaker and Howard "Hopalong" Cassady in the Ohio State locker room in 1954.

In 1955, I interviewed Michigan great and 1940 Heisman Trophy winner Tom Harmon and his wife, movie actress Elyse Knox.

Sometimes I wonder if I really have arthritis in my neck, or if it's just a permanent crick from looking up at gigantic basketball players like Wilt "the Stilt" Chamberlain.

The Aero Commander (N700KC) was the plane we used in the 1950's and 1960's for our out-of-town Ohio State football trips. The pilot (l) was Charlie Pietro. The cameraman was Denver Simmons, who accompanied me on the "Big Bear Hunt."

During the early days at Channel 4, I spent a lot of time doing commentary on the weekly pro wrestling shows televised in Columbus, Dayton and Cincinnati. Here, a wrestling favorite named Ruffy Silverstein demonstrates a hold on me.

Chief Big Heart (middle) and his father discuss the fine points of wrestling with me before a televised match in the mid-1950's. Due to hot television lights, the studio audience often endured temperatures of over 100 degrees.

In 1959, I did live commercials for my sponsor, Blatz beer. Drinking the sponsor's product on the air was optional.

In 1960, I tried unsuccessfully to coax a smile from Purdue University football coach Jack Mollenkopf prior to the Ohio State-Purdue game in Ross-Ade Stadium in West Lafayette, Indiana.

In this stand-up interview I chatted with long-time friend and OSU basketball star, Jerry Lucas.

In 1963, I spent three weeks in Sao Paulo, Brazil, covering the Pan American Games—in particular five athletes, trainers, and coaches from Columbus. I carried an Auricon sound camera, a 16 mm silent camera, and 15,000 feet of film for three half-hour shows.

Prior to the start of the 1964 Ohio State basketball season, I talked with Doug McDonald (#12), Gary Bradds (#35) and their teammates.

The look on Fred Taylor's face in 1961 seems to say, "I don't believe a word you're saying."

In 1960, the year Ohio State won the NCAA Basketball Championship, I talked with (l to r), Jerry Lucas, Fred Taylor, Larry Siegfried and Richie Hoyt.

On the set of "Echoes of Scarlet and Gray," in 1965 with Ohio State football luminaries (l to r): Ollie Cline, Carroll Widdoes, Bill Hackett, Ernie Godfrey, Bill Willis and Warren Amling.

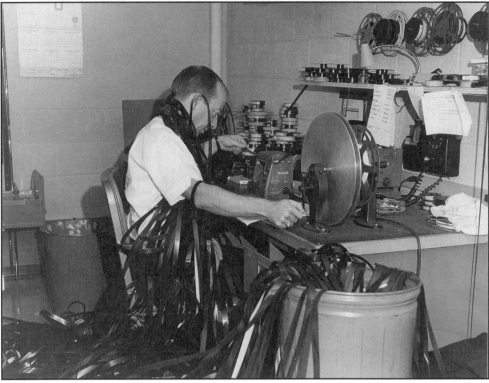

In the early 1960's, I really got wrapped up editing film of a Saturday afternoon Ohio State football game for an hour-long recap on Sunday. It was routinely an all-night job.

I wave from a convertible during WLWC day at Orient State Institute. The station's call letters were later changed to WCMH.

Here I am in the early 1960's, wearing spiked golf shoes to keep from slipping on the roof of the Walnut Hills Country Club while shooting the Ladies' PGA Tournament.

I filmed portions of a 1961 sailfishing trip to Acapulco for my outdoor show. Notice the camera in my left hand. The sailfish I landed is in the center.

Howard "Hopalong" Cassady, chatted at a soapbox derby race in the late 1950's.

Don Shula, head football coach of the Miami Dolphins, and I exchanged fashion tips during a golf outing in Columbus.

Here I am with Charlie Kemp at the Mid-Ohio Sports Car Course in the RC Cola Porsche.

I got up early to interview one of harness racing's all-time great drivers, Stanley Dancer, at Scioto Downs in the late 1970's.

Twenty-five years ago, I geared up for the ride of my life behind a harness horse at Scioto Downs.

I'm third from left and hanging on for dear life, as the horses wait for the starting gate to close.

Woody was young and handsome in 1960. Moments after this picture was taken at Channel 4, my daughter, Kelly, told him "Woody have big fat tummy."

Woody never allowed cameras inside his locker room. However, he made an exception in 1961, when he asked me to do a 30-minute recruiting film on the Buckeyes.

In 1959, when Ohio State football practices were held south of the stadium, I had many opportunities to shoot film of Woody Hayes and the Buckeyes.

At our very first Celebrity Waiters' Luncheon in 1970, Colonel John Glenn, astronaut, playfully pours coffee for Woody Hayes.

Throughout his life, Woody practiced what he preached. He always said, "You can never pay back, but you can pay forward." Here, he helped the Easter Seal Rehab Center. With us is our poster child, Michael Fullmer.

Woody Hayes always got big tips at our annual Celebrity Waiters' Luncheons.

Former OSU quarterback Tom Matte, Woody, British actress June Wilkinson, and I posed for this picture during one of our early Celebrity Waiters' Luncheons.

At a busy Celebrity Waiters' Luncheon in the 1980's, Channel 10 newscaster Dave Kaylor gets Woody's autograph while Honorary Co-chairman John Galbreath speaks.

Woody was one of the speakers who roasted and toasted me when I was honored by the Agonis Club of Columbus at its annual "Flowers for the Living" banquet.

Woody Hayes forgave my daughter Kelly for her comment at age three, "Woody have big fat tummy," and attended her wedding in 1986 to Dr. Steven Delaveris at Columbus' Greek Orthodox Church.

I was the emcee for a banquet honoring Woody in the 1980's. The guest list included (front left) Pete Rose, (rear left) Kaye Kessler, and 1950 Heisman Trophy winner Vic Janowicz.

Morganna, "the kissing bandit," has been one of the biggest crowd-pleasers and fundraisers at the annual Celebrity Waiters' Luncheon. She is a class act and a bosom buddy.

An attentive Woody Hayes, a long-time supporter of Recreation Unlimited, attended the ground-breaking ceremonies. At his left is David Ruff, son of RU founder Dick Ruff. (Photo by High Tides Photography)

Former Major League Baseball Commissioner Bowie Kuhn and I chat at the Columbus Touchdown Club.

In the early 1970's, astronaut Neil Armstrong and I worked together to raise money for the Easter Seal Society.

I hosted a post-game show for the Bengals called "Star of the Game." Featured here is Pittsburgh Steelers quarterback Terry Bradshaw.

The late Jim Trueman, founder of Red Roof Inns and TrueSports Racing, cracked me up in 1983 with a remark about the TrueSports racing team.

OSU football great Archie Griffin gets a grip on me!

This publicity photo was taken in front of the old Wyandotte Inn when I hosted the Earle Bruce TV Show in 1986.

This 1992 interview with Earle Bruce was conducted at Winding Hollow Country Club's NetCare Golf Tournament. Earle returned from Colorado to act as honorary chairman.

At the National Football Foundation and Hall of Fame banquet (Ernie Godfrey chapter), I did my 6 o'clock show live from the Ohio Union. My guest was one of the most delightful, charming, and gracious men I've ever known–the late John Galbreath, a big supporter of Recreation Unlimited.

Pro football Hall of Famer Lou "the Toe" Groza, who held sway for many years with the Cleveland Browns, paired up with me in a golf tournament at Bent Tree in 1990.

During the 1991 Sports Spectacular at Winding Hollow Country Club, former OSU basketball coach Fred Taylor presented me with the Charles Solomon Community Service Award.

I share a happy moment in 1993 with one of Columbus' most charming hostesses, LaVerne Hill.

In the early 1980's, my daughter Kelly surprised me at Halloween by dressing up as—who else?—Jimmy Crum.

In 1974, WLW Radio had just signed a new contract to continue broadcasting the Bengals' games. Phil Samp (right) was my broadcasting partner. We posed with (from left), Mike Brown, WLW-TV CEO John T. Murphy, and Paul Brown.

At Riverfront Stadium, Bengals head coach and general manager Paul Brown presented me with a plaque thanking me for my contributions to the ball club as part of the Bengals' Radio Network broadcasting team.

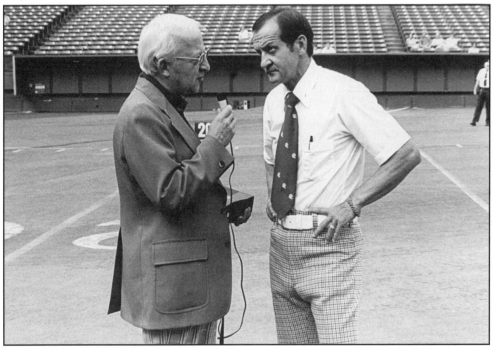

Prior to a Cincinnati Bengals home game at Riverfront Stadium, I interviewed assistant coach Rick Forzano for my pre-game broadcast.

I got together with former Pittsburgh Steelers running back Franco Harris (l) and former heavyweight boxing champion Floyd Patterson when they visited Columbus to raise funds for a local hospital.

Prior to Ohio State's 1986 Rose Bowl game in Pasadena, I visited with former Ohio State quarterbacks Ron Maciejowski (left) and Rex Kern at Rex's home in Ventura, California.

During the Ohio Glory's one year of glory, I was honored at half-time for my 40 years of broadcasting in Columbus. I provided the cheerleaders' jackets.

Here I am in 1991 with Miriam and the Captain Hans van Biljouw of Holland America's Noordam on a Recreation Unlimited cruise through Alaska's Inside Passage.

A bevy of local beauties gave me the old heave-ho before the Gold Coast Indy Car Grand Prix at Surfer's Paradise, Australia in March 1991.

Here I am at a pre-race party for the Gold Coast Indy Car Grand Prix in 1991. I'm standing with my wife, Miriam, and former Formula One Champion Alan Jones at his home on the Isle of Capri, Surfer's Paradise, Australia.

The first year at "The Old Brickyard"–Indianapolis Motor Speedway–for Jim Trueman and Bobby Rahal was one Bobby will never forget.

Cruising with me on the Recreation Unlimited Supersports Cruise in December 1987 were Indy 500 champion Robby Rahal and OSU and Boston Celtics star John Havlicek.

After presenting "Good Scout" awards to Ron Tilley, CEO of Columbia Gas, and me,
Willard Scott posed for the obligatory group picture.

On that same Recreation Unlimited cruise, Bobby Rahal and John Havlicek pose with me
and dear friend Charlie Hill, who loved wild jackets as much as I do.

Former Indy 500 champion Johnny Rutherford talked to me about the fine points of racing at the Mid-Ohio Sports Car Course in Lexington, Ohio. (Photo by MDB)

I was congratulated by Ohio Governor George Voinovich when I was inducted into the Senior Citizens' Hall of Fame in 1993.

I posed with a beautiful Crystal Tabor Fisher immediately after her wedding ceremony. She stole my heart when I met her in 1975, at the Easter Seal Rehab Center.

Mt. Vernon (Ohio) News photographer Virgil Shipley caught me with Bobby Rahal prior to the Indy Car Race at Mid-Ohio Sports Car Course in September 1991.

Indy Car driver Bobby Rahal gave me this picture shortly after he started his Rahal-Hogan racing team.

Buster Douglas posed with his grandmother at Port Columbus when he returned from Tokyo, where he had knocked out Mike Tyson to win the World Heavyweight boxing crown.

During a break in the action in surfer's Paradise, Australia, Scott Pruett, a driver for the Truesports racing team, explains the finer points of racing for the "Made in America" television special I did for Channel 4 in March 1991. The program won an Emmy.

I covered the grand opening of the Jack Nicklaus Golf Center at Kings Island in the 1970's. Here, Jack presents the high school golfer of the year award to Ralph Guarasci, as Citizen Journal sportswriter Kaye Kessler watches.

The Golden Bear and I shared a private moment during one of the early Memorial Tournaments.

Despite the fact that he has posed for thousands and thousands of pictures, Jack Nicklaus manages a sincere smile at the Ohio Union in 1989.

In 1992, I had the honor of serving as emcee for a portion of the opening ceremonies at Les Wexner's New Albany Country Club. I shared the platform with Jack Nicklaus and developer Jack Kessler.

Lee Trevino, "the Merry Mex," has been a friend for many years.

During the Pro-Am segment of the Memorial Golf Tournament, I wore a bright yellow sports coat. Lee Trevino shouted, "Well, I see you're finally wearing a coat that matches your hair!" Afterwards, we shared a laugh.

Former Ohio State quarterback Rex Kern joined me for one of our Recreation Unlimited fundraising cruises through the Caribbean.

One of the award-winners at the Columbus Touchdown Club Banquet during the 1980's was former Pittsburgh Pirates slugger Willie Stargell.

During his annual visit for the Arnold Schwarzenneger Classic, Arnold posed with me in the gym. The picture is inscribed, "Best regards to my good friend."

During a 1993 visit to Columbus for his annual body building show, my friend Arnold took time to pose with my grandson Nikolas Delaveris.

Dick Ruff, founder of Recreation Unlimited, (second from right) looks characteristically modest as he is photographed by TV 4 photographer Stan Phillipi.

As Founding Chairman of Ohio Special Olympics, I had the pleasure of introducing Eunice Kennedy Shriver at the opening of the Ohio Special Olympics State Summer Games in Ohio Stadium in the early 1980's.

Dave Thomas, founder of Wendy's and a major supporter of Recreation Unlimited, spoke at ground-breaking ceremonies as Don Hughes and David Cassady look on.

Ribbon-cutting ceremonies at Recreation Unlimited camp—a dream becomes a reality. (Photo by High Tides Photography)

This is an aerial view of the Recreation Unlimited camp, located south of Ashley in Delaware County. At left is Lake Crum, named in my honor by the Central Ohio RV and Marine Dealers. They've been great supporters of RU.

I congratulate RU camper Karen Fritz on her performance of "You Are the Wind Beneath My Wings" at the grand opening of the Recreation Unlimited camp. (Photo by High Tides Photography)

At the first Celebrity Waiters' Luncheon in 1972, Colonel John Glenn was one of our waiters. He posed here with me and Columbus insurance executives Dick McCann and Art Zang, who were instrumental in getting Recreation Unlimited off the ground.

Charlie Hill's daughter and Miriam share a moment with Scioto Downs publicity director Chuck Stokes, Ohio State basketball star Larry Bolden, and Scioto Downs founder Charlie Hill at the first Celebrity Waiters' Luncheon.

John Glenn, Miriam, and a close friend, Sally Davis, talked over old times during one of the early Celebrity Waiters' Luncheons.

The greatest gatherings of OSU athletes and coaches, past and present, occurred at Celebrity Waiters' Luncheons. Back row (l to r), Art Schlichter, Larry Bolden, Hugh Hindman, Clark Kellogg, Earle Bruce and Ray Griffin. In the background are Governor Jim Rhodes, me, and Hugh DeMoss. Front row (l to r), Pete Johnson, Eldon Miller, Dave Mainwaring, (who paid $1,000 to Celebrity Waiters to have the picture taken), Archie Griffin, Steve Luke, Kelvin Ransey, Bill Hoskett and Greg Lashutka.

In 1975, five-year-old Suzi Solomon, born without arms and legs, was the Princess of the Longhorn Rodeo at the Fairgrounds Coliseum. A portion of the rodeo's proceeds went to the Easter Seals Rehab Center, where Suzi was a client.

Seventeen years later, in 1992, Suzi Solomon graduated from Wright State University with a degree in hospital administration. That same year, she and I posed for this picture.

I'm surrounded here by some of my "special children" at a cookout I had at my home.

Julie Rogers joined me at the 1984 Easter Seal Telethon. I met Julie in 1955.

Stacey Wiggins from Circleville, another long-time friend from the Easter Seal Rehab Center, joined me during the 1984 Easter Seal Telethon. In 1993, I delivered the commencement address when Stacey graduated from Brooks-Yates School in Circleville.

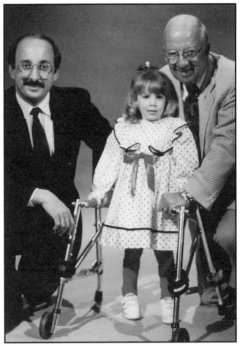

I got a smooch from Tristan Marie Renat at the 1992 Easter Seal Telethon. On the back of this picture, Tristan wrote, "Hi, Jimmy. I love you!" This makes it all worthwhile.

Bobby Rahal, honorary chairman of the Easter Seal Telethon for 8 years, posed in 1990 with poster child Erica Atwood and me.

Here I am with two other beautiful Easter Seal friends. (Photography by Larry Phillips Photography)

Arnold Schwarzenneger and his wife, Maria Shriver, joined me on the set during several Easter Seal Telethons.

During our 1990 National Easter Seal Telethon meeting in Las Vegas, I posed with my local telethon co-host, P.J. Ryal (left rear), and national co-hosts Mary Frann, Rob Weller and Pat Boone.

Daughter Kelly brought my grandchildren Nikolas, Michalea and Manny to the 1990 Easter Seal Telethon.

Art Schlichter, former Ohio State quarterback, cheerfully answered phones during the 1984 Easter Seal Telethon.

I received a farewell hug from National Telethon co-host Mary Frann at the National Easter Seal Telethon meeting at the Beverly Hilton (California) Hotel in January 1993.

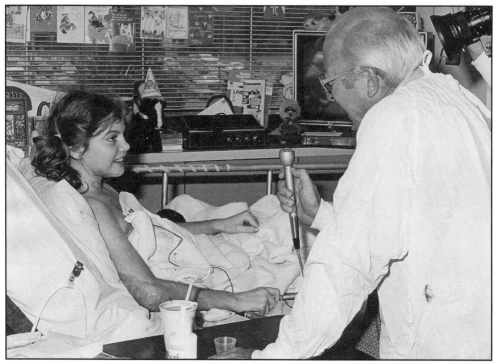

In September, 1976, I visited with Belinda Munday in Children's Hospital Burn Unit while videotaping segments for the documentary, "Three Tower North," which won an Emmy. The photographer is Bruce Johansson.

Here I am with Easter Seal Telethon national host Pat Boone–in Las Vegas in 1985. He is ageless.

Belinda Munday and I visited a baby llama at the Columbus Zoo in 1977 during one of her trips to Columbus from her home in Parkersburg, West Virginia.

Jessica Stewart waters a plant while her twin sister Jennifer smiles for the camera. I met Jessica at Children's Hospital in the fall of 1986, and visited her nearly every day during the six months before she died. This photo was taken in 1985 when the twins were 8.

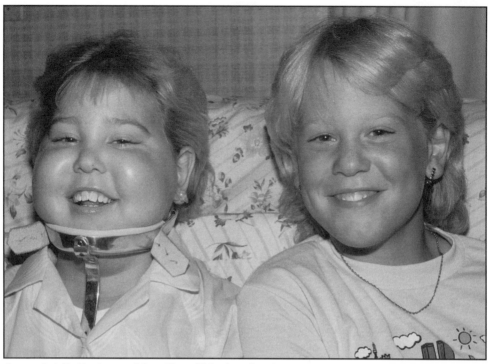

At age 9 1/2, Jessica and Jennifer still had smiles that could bring you to your knees.

Jessica and Jennifer Stewart and their parents, Bob and Cindy Grewell, were in Florida in 1986 while Kelly McCormick and I were there for an international diving competition. Kelly visited with Jessica (left) and presented her with the gold medal she won in three-meter diving competition. Jessica died in 1987.

I photographed Ohio State divers Kelly McCormick and Mary Ellen Clark taking a wombat break at the world-famous Sydney Zoo prior to the 1988 Olympics.

Four years later, while touring Australia in 1992 prior to the Indy Car Grand Prix, it was my turn to hold a wombat.

Channel 4 photographer Tim Moushey holds the camera as I interview Kelly McCormick and Chinese diver Gao Min in Sydney, Australia. Gao was an Olympic gold medalist in women's three-meter diving in the 1988 Olympic games. Kelly took the bronze. In Sydney, Gao placed first and Kelly, second.

Kelly McCormick Robertson proudly shows off her daughter, Alexandra Patricia, born September 20, 1992.

*Kelly McCormick in action! She won a silver medal in the
1984 Olympics and a bronze medal in 1988.*

*Kelly's mother, Pat McCormick, won double gold medals in plat-
form and springboard diving in the 1952 and 1956 Olympics.*

On the first tee at Muirfield President Ford stands with a Crummy announcer.

I thought Bob Hope might never give the bullhorn back after I introduced him on the first tee at Muirfield. A smiling Jack Nicklaus (left) waits to tee off.

In 1985 I met with President Ronald Reagan in the oval office. My wife and I were accompanied by Congressman John Kasich; I presented the President with a personalized OSU football jersey prepared for me by OSU equipment manager John Bozick.

I waved to friends at the 1993 Upper Arlington 4th of July parade. I was honored to be grand marshal. (Photo by Upper Arlington This Week)

Kelly brightened up the night with her vocal renditions at a 1993 Pops concert.

Our fifth grandchild, Carl, shown here with mother Kelly, was born in the spring of 1993.

Our 1991 Christmas card picture featured four of our grandchildren (l to r) Nikolas, Michalea, Manny and Nathan.

This caricature says it all. How 'bout that?

7

Why Did I Say That About John Cooper?

When John Cooper signed on as Ohio State's head football coach on December 31, 1987, he brought with him a solid record of achievements.

As head coach at Arizona State he had led the Sun Devils to a PAC-10 title—a first for the school—a Rose Bowl victory over Michigan, and a record of 10 wins, 1 loss and 1 tie during the 1986 season.

In 1986 he was also named National Coach of the Year. During his three years with the Sun Devils, Cooper's overall record of wins, losses, and ties was, respectively, 25-9-2. Before taking the post at Arizona State, Cooper had been for eight years head coach at Tulsa, where the Golden Hurricane had six straight winning seasons.

Cooper's record was impressive, but I think the Rose Bowl victory over Michigan probably carried the most weight with Ohio State. Ironically, Cooper's teams lost to Michigan the first four seasons he came to Ohio State, and tied 13-13 in his fifth year. With the Buckeyes' fourth consecutive loss during the 1991-92 season, Cooper became the first coach in seventy years to lose four straight to the Wolverines. (John Wilce beat Cooper's poor showing by two—Wilce's teams lost six in a row between 1922 and 1927.)

The 28-point loss in 1991 to Michigan (Michigan 31, OSU-3) also set another record of sorts—it was the Wolverines' biggest win over the Bucks since 1946, when Michigan posted a 58-6 win.

If you didn't know before from my sports commentaries, you have probably concluded that I am not a big John Cooper fan. In my opinion, Cooper did a terrible job his first three seasons, then committed the unpardonable sin in his fourth season of losing yet again to Michigan, and didn't do much better his fifth season with the 13-13 tie.

His coaching style, too, leaves a lot to be desired. First of all, he came in and referred to himself as an "administrative coach." His philosophy is, "I coach the assistant coaches and the assistant coaches coach the players."

I have stood with John Cooper along the sidelines at practice sessions where he'd spend 30 to 45 minutes talking to reporters and friends, without once looking over to see what was happening on the field. Now, how is a coach going to know what his players are doing—how they're acting and reacting—when he doesn't consistently watch them during practice?

I shared this concern with Moose Machinsky, captain of the 1957 Ohio State team. Moose's response was, "My God! When I played for Woody, he knew every move that every player was supposed to make on every play. If a player screwed up in a practice session, he'd send us on a quarter-mile run from the old practice field down to the Olentangy River."

I had watched many of Woody's practices, and I knew Moose was right. Unlike Woody, who was a "hands-on" coach, during his first five years John Cooper was a "hands-off" coach. That's my number one "unofficial" criticism.

The first official criticism I leveled was for his decision to quit when he was behind after a severe thunderstorm caused play to be suspended during the USC-Ohio State Game in 1990. Here's a condensed version of what I said during my sports commentary on October 1, 1990:

"A few weeks ago, prior to an Ohio State football practice at the Woody Hayes facility, Buckeye boss John Cooper told me that the trouble with people in Columbus is that they live too much in the past.

"Well, maybe they do. But having covered Woody Hayes for all of his twenty-eight colorful and controversial years, I know one thing—Wayne Woodrow would never have called it quits with two minutes and 36 seconds left in the game . . . regardless of the score. Nor would the World War II naval officer have told the enemy where he was going to strike next. That's not the way you play the game.

"When I asked Cooper at today's media luncheon why he chose to call it quits instead of going along with what the referee suggested—suspension— the first thing I got was an icy stare, followed by a convoluted reply . . . .

"Ohio State players, knowing that anything can happen—witness games in the last two years against LSU and Minnesota—wanted to play those final two minutes and 36 seconds, but they were not given the chance to do so, because of a coach who decided to quit."

I did not endear myself to Coach Cooper with that commentary, but that wasn't my purpose. I spoke for many fans when I criticized his decision to quit. But obviously the fans' opinions didn't cut any ice with Cooper.

I gave my commentary on a Monday night. On Tuesday, John Cooper came looking for me at the TV station. He arrived about half an hour before I was due in, and rather than wait, told the switchboard operator to tell me he'd be back.

We had a relief switchboard operator on duty that day. Brian usually works in the mailroom and he's got a pretty good sense of humor, which he tried out on John Cooper. He hadn't heard my commentary, though, and he didn't know Cooper was mad.

Anyhow, as Cooper was walking away, Brian called out, "Coach, before you leave, will you give me the Big Bear wave?" Brian later said that if looks could kill, he would have fallen dead on the spot!

Cooper came back the next day and we met behind closed doors for about an hour. Among other things, he told me he didn't appreciate being called a quitter. I said, "Coop, I didn't call you a quitter. You called yourself a quitter at the press conference right after the game. I've got the tape right here."

I turned on the videotape and it showed another reporter asking, "Coach, what does suspension [of the game] mean to you?"

Cooper replied, "It means you suspend the game until the weather improves and then you continue . . . . but I told the official who came over to tell me they were going to suspend the game with only two minutes and 36 seconds to go, 'Let's do the kickoff. If we don't get the ball, there will be nothing we can do, so we'll call it quits.'"

I stopped the tape and said, "Mr. Cooper, you called yourself a quitter. If nothing else, you gave up on your players and that's worse than being a quitter. You failed to remember a year ago when you were behind Minnesota 31-0 and came back and won the game."

Several weeks later, when Cooper asked for a contract extension as a vote of confidence, I felt compelled to speak up again and voice what I knew were the views of many loyal but disgusted Ohio State fans. My commentary follows.

"Now as to the possibility of Ohio State University extending the contract of Coach John Cooper, who is finishing the third of a five-year contract—come on, folks, let's get serious!

"Let's say you're a businessman and you've just lost your biggest account of the year for the third time in as many years. [I am referring here to the third straight loss to Michigan.] *Are you going to extend the contract of the man who handled that account? I think that answer would be a resounding "No!" in 99 out of 100 cases.*

"You're going to sit down and evaluate that man's overall performance and, perhaps, look ahead to the fourth year of a five-year contract. If, next year, he can avoid problems with the Trojans and Hoosiers and, finally, land that big account from up north—then and only then do you sit down and start talking about a contract extension.

"Now is not the time to even think about extending the contract of a man who at the management level refuses to take any of the blame for a transaction that failed . . . . choosing, instead, to put the blame on the people who work for him—citing 'poor execution" as the reason for the failure.'

"Management cannot continue to put the blame on those who gave it everything they had but came up short.

"Good management leads to good execution. Poor management leads to poor execution, and the loss of another big account.

"Contract extension? Next year, perhaps, but not now."

Two days later, OSU President Gordon Gee said he wouldn't even talk about a contract extension until after the fourth year of the contract. So, obviously, in my commentary I spoke for a lot of people. The thing that put the capper on my relationship with John Cooper, however, concerned an occurrence at the 1990 Liberty Bowl in Memphis.

As you may recall, the Buckeyes lost 23-11 to Air Force—a team they outmanned in every way. How did this happen?

The day before the game, John Cooper took his team to a breakfast that had been planned for them by Liberty Bowl officials. Then he took them to a luncheon and, afterwards, he bused them out to the Liberty Bowl stadium and let them walk around. Then he took them back to the hotel. That was it.

That same day, I went over to cover Air Force. Their middle linebacker was Brian Hill, whose father, Billy Hill, is head trainer for Ohio State. I was preparing a story about a father and son on different sides of the fence.

What a contrast there was to Ohio State in how Air Force spent the day before the Liberty Bowl! The Air Force team was in full pads—not hitting hard, but suited up. Later, Air Force Coach Fisher DeBerry let me listen in when he called his players into a huddle. After reminding them of some general things about the trip, he got serious.

"Gentlemen," he told them, "tomorrow you're going to play one of the top football teams in the country. Year in and year out, they are dynamite. Their coach, John Cooper, is a friend of mine—and he's an outstanding coach.

"As you know, this game is being dedicated to the Armed Forces in Saudia Arabia and, as the Air Force team, you are part of that operation. When you get back to your rooms, I want you to put your game faces on. I want you to get focused. And when you get on the field tomorrow, remember that this is war!"

I got goose bumps listening to DeBerry's talk. I thought about it later during the game, when it became crystal clear which team was motivated and which was not.

Following Ohio State's dismal performance at the Liberty Bowl, I returned to Columbus and prepared yet another commentary on John Cooper. It aired on December 28, 1990.

"Today, as I returned from the Liberty Bowl, I ran into a former Ohio

State football player at Port Columbus. He played for Woody Hayes and, later, for Vince Lombardi.

"He agreed with my thoughts that any team is a direct reflection of the head coach. The coach's intensity, desire, work habits, his planning and execution—those things rub off on the players. At least, they should! When they're missing in the coach, you won't find them on the field.

"Most of those ingredients were missing last night in Memphis. And, although I didn't see last night's Ohio State basketball game, I would have to think that—based on Randy Ayers' approach to coaching basketball—those ingredients were very much in evidence as the basketball Buckeyes performed the way an Ohio State athletic team is expected to perform.

"In forty years of covering Ohio State football, I've been exposed to practically every situation, under every set of circumstances, you can expect to find in college football.

"I have great respect for the members of the Ohio State football squad. They're fine athletes—honest, straightforward, dedicated, hardworking, and very intelligent. But never have I seen an Ohio State team as outclassed, outhustled, outplayed, and outcoached as the one that took the field last night against the Falcons. That's a reflection on the coach and the coaching—and shouldn't be happening to a great university like Ohio State . . .

"I said when John Cooper was hired that it takes four years for a new coach to get everything in place—his own staff, the players he's recruited. It takes that much time to build a winning program.

"Right now, there are many who doubt that he can get the job done, and I may be one of those Doubting Thomases. But I'm willing to give him and his coaches—including the new ones who'll be joining his staff in the next few days—another eleven months to do what his good friend, Air Force Coach Fisher DeBerry, did last night in Memphis—and that is to put a team on the field that will not be an embarrassment to one of the greatest universities in the United States."

In all fairness to John Cooper, I tore into him three times in three months—probably as hard as anybody had done in the state of Ohio—but when it came time to help with the Easter Seal Telethon in March of 1991, he was there to do his part. He couldn't attend the Celebrity Waiters'

Luncheon in May, but he was courteous enough to call me well in advance and asked that I let him know which of his players I wanted to wait tables to raise funds for Recreation Unlimited.

In terms of the following year's performance, the Buckeyes' 1991 record of 8-4 was a disappointment—especially the 31-3 loss to Michigan. The Bucks did move up from a fifth to a third place finish in the Big Ten Conference. Still, reporters were flabbergasted at the three-year contract extension granted to Cooper by OSU President Gordon Gee—an extension that was announced half an hour before the Wolverines stomped the Buckeyes.

Gee's move left most fans' jaws on the floor, too. Remember, Cooper had asked for and been denied a contract extension in 1990 after his third season. And, until the university's press release was distributed announcing the surprising news, Gee had said over and over that he wouldn't make a decision about extending Cooper's contract until the regular season had ended.

The only rationale I can guess at is that Ohio State bungled so badly in the firing of Earle Bruce that the university wanted to avoid more bad press. Ironically, that's just what it got.

The bad press continued throughout the 1992 season, in which Ohio State had a overall record of 8-3-1, with a 5-2-1 record in the Big Ten. Following their 13-13 tie with Michigan, the team lost 21-14 to Georgia in the Citrus Bowl.

Typical of what was being said and written about Cooper during the season was a headline in the November 19, 1992 *Columbus Dispatch*: "Two Losses Could Cost Cooper His Job."

"John Cooper is not expected to survive as Ohio State's football coach if he loses a fifth straight time to Michigan and a fourth straight bowl game, high-placed university officials told the *Dispatch*. . . ." The article continued, "Sources indicate Cooper's status has created divisiveness within the university, the community and the alumni."

An *Akron Beacon-Journal* article written in October, 1992, by columnist Steve Love stated, "Cooper is the embodiment of Peter's most famous principle: In a hierarchy, every employee tends to rise to his level of incompetence."

Obviously, I'm not the only journalist with a less than positive opinion of the man. I once again shared my own feelings about John Cooper's performance as a coach in an October 12 commentary based on on-camera remarks he made to me during a press conference following the 20-16 loss to Wisconsin on October 5th. Cooper's words were: "We're not good enough to win on an off day." After showing a tape of Cooper's comments, here's what I said on the air.

"This is an open letter to Ohio State President Gordon Gee and Athletic Director Jim Jones . . . .
Gentlemen:

"The time has come for you two to begin searching for a new football coach at The Ohio State University. Speaking not only for myself but for thousands of loyal Buckeye followers who are now disappointed and discontented, I'm requesting that you ask for the resignation of football coach John Cooper, appoint an interim head coach to restructure what's left of a season that's become an embarrassment, and begin a search for a head coach who can give the athletes who represent Ohio State much more than they are getting at the present time.

"The young men wearing the scarlet and gray are quality individuals, but they're getting something less than quality leadership. Talentwise, Ohio State's football team is like a great symphonic orchestra—but they can't play a note because they have no director.

"I've debated with myself for quite some time about whether or not to say what I'm saying tonight, but John Cooper forced my hand with his remark following the loss to Wisconsin. What this Ohio State football team needs is positive reinforcement, not a head coach who says 'We're not good enough to win on an off-day.'

"These players read newspapers, watch TV and listen to the radio. Sooner or later, after hearing their coach say 'We're not good enough,' they're going to start thinking that way. Instead of listening to a head coach who's inspirational, who's supposed to light the fire in their bellies, they're being told they're not good enough, and before long they'll begin to believe it.

"Woody Hayes always told his players they could be as good as they wanted to be, that even on an off-day if they had the guts, the desire, the spirit and the intensity that Buckeyes are supposed to have, they could win. And 76.1 percent of the time Woody was head coach, they were winners.

"That was because of great leadership—not because of a coach who said, 'We're not good enough to win an an off-day.'

"Earlier this year, John Cooper said time and time again: 'We have to improve so we can get Ohio State football back to the level it was at before I became head coach.'

"True, John Cooper did not fumble. Nor did he miss a field goal that helped Illinois beat Ohio State for the fifth straight year. But by the same token, players who've been properly motivated, players who've been inspired, players who've been instilled with confidence by their head coach—these players don't have that much to worry about if those things happen. Because even on an off day, they'll find a way to win.

"It was time for a change after John Cooper lost four straight to Illinois and Michigan. Now that changing of the guard becomes even more imperative. Without a change, the program will continue to suffer. The young men representing Ohio State on the football field deserve much more than mediocrity.

"They deserve a chance to come out of a game—win or lose—with their heads held high. With no director, that symphonic orchestra is on the verge of becoming a string quartet.

"The winning tradition, Scarlet and Gray, Buckeye battle cry, the victory bell in the stadium tower—they've disappeared. They're gone.

"Gordon Gee and Jim Jones, how long can you turn your backs on a situation that's become deplorable? The ball is in your court. The next move is yours. Like thousands of loyal Buckeyes around the world, I await your answer.

Sincerely, Jimmy Crum"

I got a lot of public support for my comments. *The Other Paper*, a news and entertainment weekly, even coined a new verb for my criticism—"crummed." Their headline for the October 15-21, 1992 issue was "CRUMMED! Jimmy Blitzes Coop."

When John Elsasser, a reporter for *The Other Paper*, called Athletic Director Jim Jones for his response to my commentary, Jones told him: "I have no response to Jimmy's commentary. I didn't hear it, at either 6 or 11."

To this day, I haven't heard a word from Jim Jones. I did, however, have a lengthy conversation with OSU President Gordon Gee after the 1992 football season was over. Gordon invited me to fly with him on the university plane to an alumni meeting in Indianapolis to see my son, Jim, who was then president of that city's Ohio State Alumni Club.

There were seven on us on the plane and the moment the plane took off, Gordon, who was across the aisle from me, said "Okay, now let's talk about John Cooper, Woody Hayes and Earle Bruce. But, remember, anything that's said in this airplane is strictly off the record."

We had a lengthy conversation—one that cleared the air for me—on the trip to and from Indianapolis. And, true to my word, it remains strictly off the record.

I will say that it wasn't easy or fun to write the commentaries I wrote about John Cooper. I did what I felt I had to do. I knew that Channel 10 wasn't going to say anything, because they produce Cooper's TV show. I knew that guys at Channel 6 didn't have the rank to feel they could speak up. If something was going to be said, I was the only one with the experience and longevity to do it.

As this book goes to press, the beginning of the 1993 football season is only a few days away and things are looking brighter for John Cooper and the Buckeyes. There's no question that the talent on the 1993 team is equal to, if not better than, anything the Buckeyes have had in many years. If talent alone could win football games, this team could be headed for national prominence.

But talent isn't enough. Achieving national prominence requires a cohesiveness of purpose that starts at the very top. And that's where I've seen the biggest improvement this fall. I've seen a different John Cooper on the practice field at the Woody Hayes facility. He's been a "hands on" coach—criticizing his players when things go wrong and praising them when things go according to the play book.

I've seen him yelling and hollering in practices this year, doing what's necessary to motivate some very talented players. Perhaps John Cooper has finally decided to practice what Woody Hayes preached: "You win with people." This could very well be the year that Cooper finishes the season with more Ohio State friends than enemies.

I hope so.

8

♦

Bobby Knight and
Other Pals

O f all the friends I've made in this business, only Bobby
Knight rivals Woody Hayes for controversy. Woody lived long enough to
be considered an old softie. So far, Bob hasn't put in enough time on earth
to live down his reputation as a tough guy, but I predict he will. Bobby's
former players admire and respect him, but—as with Woody Hayes—the
general public either loves him or hates him.

Bobby has a reputation for being hard to get along with, but there's
always a method to his madness. Most of the time, it has to do with looking out for the welfare of his players. And the guy has a great sense of
humor—one that he uses shamelessly to one-up his friends. As the
following story illustrates, Bobby has gotten me more than once with his
practical jokes.

A few days before the Indiana-Ohio State game here in Columbus
during the 1989-90 season, Bobby called me to set up a pre-game interview. We set a date for the night before the game, and he arrived at the
WCMH studio about 10:30 p.m. for a live 11:00 p.m. interview. The

interview went well, and Bobby behaved just as graciously and politely as he always does to his friends. His concluding on-air comment was, "Anytime I can do anything to help you, Jim, just let me know. It's been a pleasure to talk with you."

After Bobby left, I wrapped up the news and then stopped back at my desk to pick up some things before I went home. Just as I got there, the phone rang. A voice said, "Hey, Crum, it's the Dragon. Did the alarm go off?"

"You didn't say anything on the air to make alarms go off!" I kidded back, knowing from the voice and nickname that Bob Knight was on the line.

"That's right," he responded. "But I noticed a sign when I was leaving the TV station that said 'If you leave this door open for more than 60 seconds, an alarm will sound.' So I stuck a phone book in the door."

When I checked it out, I learned that the alarm had mysteriously gone off. Bobby Knight had struck again!

No one has ever accused the man of being shy. Bobby has been in the limelight since becoming head coach at the University of Indiana in 1971. (This followed six years of coaching at West Point.) By 1976, he had led the Hoosiers to their 200th victory (93-56 over Georgia).

In 1979, he coached the U.S. Pan American team that won a gold medal. Five years later, he coached the U.S. Olympic team that took the gold medal in Los Angeles. Back at Indiana, he won his 500th victory in 1989—this one a 92-76 win over Northwestern—and became the winningest coach in Big Ten history. Under Knight's tutelage, the Hoosiers have racked up one, two, three, four and five-year Big Ten records for most wins. In 26 years, Bobby Knight's teams have had just one losing season.

Bobby was Big Ten Coach of the Year in 1973, 1975, and 1976. He was named Naismith Coach of the Year in 1987 and National Coach of the Year in 1989. This past year he was elected to the Basketball Hall of Fame. Despite the periodic rumors that he's considering another offer, Bob has remained steadfastly loyal to Indiana. He's often said Indiana is an ideal situation for him and that his loyalty has gotten stronger the longer he remains at the school.

Yes, Bob Knight has thrown a few chairs in his time. And he's made plenty of sports reporters mad. For years, I've been the only sports anchor in Columbus he'll give an interview to.

I think the years have mellowed him, but apparently Bobby doesn't. He continues to stir up plenty of controversy. A recent "scandal" was his "use" of a bullwhip on players—a sign of Bobby's offbeat humor and not a racist act, as some in the press would have you believe. Even his own black players said the charges of racism were ridiculous.

It's true Bobby has a temper, and it's one that rivals Woody's in intensity. But, like Woody, Bob Knight also has loyalty, patience, and a true genius for coaching—a skill he has generously shared with others.

More than a dozen of his assistant coaches and former players are now head coaches themselves. Like Woody, Bobby's foremost concern has always been that his players get an education. To his immense credit, 95 percent of them have gotten their degrees. I am proud to call Bobby Knight my friend.

* * * *

Any balanced discussion of Art Schlichter must begin with a review of his impressive record. One of Ohio State's most talented quarterbacks, Art was a starter in every game from 1978 through 1981. Of 951 passes attempted, he completed 497, for 7,547 yards and 50 touchdowns. Art played in four Bowl games (Gator Bowl, 1978; Rose Bowl, 1979; Fiesta Bowl, 1980; and the Liberty Bowl in 1981). He was named Most Valuable Player in the Big Ten in 1981. And yet, when you ask people to say the word they associate with Art Schlichter, it's not "football," it's "gambling."

I first became aware of Art's gambling habit in 1983 when Art, Woody Hayes and I flew to Ft. Myers, Florida, to participate in a Celebrity Waiters' Luncheon to raise money for the American Lung Association of Southwest Florida. I had been asked to serve as master of ceremonies for the event, and I took Woody and Art—then a quarterback for the Baltimore Colts—along as waiters. Art had been a first-round draft pick in 1982. Woody and I, along with everyone else who knew him, thought Art had the world by the tail.

The Lung Association put the three of us up in a condominium in North Ft. Myers. After we dropped off our luggage, Art and I met some people for a golf date. Before we teed off, Art suggested we make a friendly bet on the game. I agreed and, until later, didn't give it a second thought.

The three of us had a great couple of days together. In retrospect, Woody and I both remembered hearing Art on the phone late at night but thought he was talking to Maria, the Ohio State cheerleader he dated.

We learned later that Art was on the phone to the FBI, asking them for protection when we returned to Columbus. He told reporters he feared for his life because of $389,000 in gambling debts he owed to some Maryland bookies who wouldn't think twice about taking it out of his hide.

When we found out that his late night phone calls had to do with gambling and not romance, Woody and I were two very surprised people! We had just spent forty-eight hours with Art, and neither of us had suspected he had a care in the world.

Woody, of course, was deeply hurt to learn what was going on with Art. He had taken great pride in Art's achievements, and was surprised and disappointed. However, true to form, he remained loyal.

Earle Bruce, who'd coached Art through his last three seasons, was just as surprised as Woody. "I like to watch the horses run. I play a little cards, but I don't understand this. I'm out of my element. I think anyone who bets on football or basketball is crazy," Earle said, adding, "He made a mistake, but Art is still a Buckeye."

That sums up my feelings, too. As everybody knows, Art's troubles were not over quickly. After his gambling debts came to light, the National Football League suspended Art for 13 months because of his gambling activities. Art admitted some of his bets were on NFL games but said he never bet on any Colts games.

In the late spring of 1983 he checked into a gambling rehabilitation program in Amityville, New York, for treatment but, as it turned out, was not able at that time to beat the addiction. Art rejoined the Colts in 1984 but was cut in 1985. He played briefly for the Buffalo Bills in 1986.

In 1987, he was arrested on misdemeanor charges of sports gambling in Indianapolis after wagering more than $270,000 in two-and-a-half months. In 1988, he filed for bankruptcy in Columbus. Two days later, Art signed a one-year contract as a quarterback with the Ottowa Rough Riders of the Canadian Football League.

He lost that job after two games, was brought back later in the season when the Rough Riders changed head coaches, then was sidelined with a rib injury before being let go. He later played for the Detroit Drive in 1990-91. In between and since, he's worked for a car dealership, as a radio sports announcer, and as a rep for an athletic equipment manufacturing company. He's now employed as a radio talk show host at WSAI Radio in Cincinnati.

Just recounting Art's problems is exhausting. Imagine living through them firsthand! Art said he got caught up in gambling back in college for one big reason—to relieve the constant pressure he felt to excell.

To this day, Art Schlichter is a good friend of mine. He made a million dollar mistake, but he's straightened out his life. To show you the kind of guy Art was even when he was in trouble: I had taken Art with me to Children's Hospital to meet a young man named Scotty Siersma who had developed cancer and was in serious shape. He's now recovered and lives here in Columbus, where I see him quite often.

After meeting Scotty once before going off to the Colts training camp back in 1982, Art called me and asked for Scotty's phone number so he could hear firsthand how he was doing. Scotty, of course, was thrilled. He and his family still talk about that phone call from Art Schlichter.

* * * *

A friend who's never had even a breath of scandal in his life is Jack Nicklaus. Few people will argue with me when I say Jack exemplifies all that's great about golf. He's a fine sportsman as well as one of pro golf's career leaders, with more than $5 million in PGA earnings. Jack has made millions more designing golf courses all over the world.

The Golden Bear won his first professional event in 1962, his first year on the PGA Tour, and he's been winning them ever since. Back then, he was known as the big, chubby kid from Ohio State, where he enrolled after graduating from Upper Arlington High School in 1958. He'd won the U.S. Amateur in 1959 at age 19 and in 1960 was runner-up at the U.S. Open, competing as an amateur. From then on, Jack's career has continued to be legendary. Now over 50, he's still hanging in there and winning on the Senior PGA Tour.

The involvement of Jack and his wife, Barbara, in charities is legendary, also. A few years ago, Jack called and said Barbara had been in Columbus over the weekend—they've made their home in North Palm Beach,

Florida for years. She'd heard me talking on Channel 4 about Recreation Unlimited, and wanted to learn more about it.

I sent a videotape and some literature showing how the program helps to maximize the potential of children with special needs. I heard nothing for a long time, then one morning I got a call from Jack saying he and Barbara wanted to become supporters. Each year since, Recreation Unlimited has received a sizeable check at Christmas.

This past July, I received a letter from Jack expressing his regrets at not being able to attend the Jimmy Crum Tribute held at Villa Milano. An excerpt from his letter reads:

"I'm sorry my tournament schedule does not allow me to join you this evening as Ohio pays tribute to one of its foremost sports authorities and humanitarians. Jimmy, this is a good chance for me to thank you for all the years of support you have given me. You've been a great friend, not only to me, but to the Memorial Tournament. I can't think of anyone else who is more deserving of this tribute. . . Barbara joins me in sending you best wishes for a wonderful evening."

Jack has always been a family man—maybe that's because he grew up in such a close one. His dad, Charlie, who passed away in the late 1970's, ran the Nicklaus Drug Store in Columbus for years and years. He and Jack were extremely close and, like Jack, Charlie had a good sense of humor.

I often shopped at his drug store and will never forget the laugh Charlie and I shared about my complexion following a Florida vacation. I had spent a lot of time out in the sun and have a tendency to get more of a sunburn than a suntan.

It seems Charlie had watched me on the news the night before and was upset because my color was so red. "I spent half an hour trying to get the red out of my TV set while you were on the air last night," he told me. "But every time I did, I got a black and white set!"

* * * *

Another golfer I've always liked a lot is Tom Weiskopf, who still holds a share of the OSU Scarlet course record, an 8 under par 64. The year of the first Memorial Tournament at Muirfield, while I was at the course covering the early arrivals, Tom was on the seventh fairway (a par 5), hitting approach shots to the green.

For a school assignment, my son, Jim, happened to be "shadowing" me that day to see what I really did for a living. He was 15 at the time, and went on to get a broadcast journalism degree Ohio State. He later got a law degree and now practices in Carmel, Indiana.

Anyhow, Jim was quite happy to be at Muirfield instead of at school, and was thrilled when Tom Weiskopf motioned for us to join him on the fairway. When he asked Jim what kind of shots he should hit into the green, Jim was even more thrilled. Tom Weiskopf has one of the finest swings in the game, yet he was kind enough to ask a fifteen-year-old what kind of shots he wanted to see.

Later, when we returned to the clubhouse, Jack Nicklaus invited us to join him for lunch. After lunch we went to Port Columbus to do an interview with Arnold Palmer. While we were waiting for Arnold to arrive, we ran into Paul Tibbetts, who piloted the Enola Gay and dropped the bomb on Hiroshima, ending World War II.

When he reported on the "day in the life of a broadcast journalist" to his class, Jim Jr. had a hard time convincing his classmates that he had really met Weiskopf, Nicklaus and all the others on the very same day!

* * * *

Tom Weiskopf's coach at Ohio State was Bob Kepler, who also coached Jack Nicklaus. When Kepler left Ohio State, he became the golf pro at Hound's Ear in North Carolina.

Several years ago, when Miriam and I spent a couple of days in North Carolina with the Keplers, Bob told me that Nicklaus and Weiskopf were so talented that he never tried to teach them anything. Instead, he said he simply tried to improve on their God-given talents.

He shared this story about Weiskopf with me: Tom once called him at Hound's Ear after a Pro-Am at the Greensboro Open Golf Tournament in Greensboro, North Carolina, and told Bob he'd played so poorly in the Pro Am that he was going to withdraw from the tournament.

Kepler knew Tom's swing so well that he was able to diagnose what was wrong just from their phone conversation. He told Tom what to do to remedy the situation and convinced him to hang in there. In Bob's words, "I gave him a twenty minute golf lesson on the phone."

A reporter for a Charlotte TV station happened to hear Bob's end of the phone conversation. When Bob hung up, the reporter asked him to appear on his TV show that night. "The guy had a ten-minute sports show and he devoted half of it to the lesson I'd given Weiskopf on the phone," Bob recalled.

The next day, Weiskopf shot a 66 and took the first-round lead in the Greensboro Open. With a big smile on his face, Bob told me, "Everyone who'd watched that sports show on WBT-TV thought I was the greatest coach in the world 'cause I'd given Tom a phone lesson and he'd gone on to take the first-round lead."

* * * *

One of the nicest women I've met in the world of sports is Kathy Whitworth, who is also one of the greatest golfers on the LPGA circuit. She won her first tournament in 1962 and, since then, has won more tournaments—88 at last count—than anyone, male or female, in golf history. (Next on the history list are Sam Snead, with 81 victories on the PGA tour, and Jack Nicklaus with 71.)

The Associated Press named Kathy Woman Athlete of the Year in 1965 and 1967. She led the Ladies' Professional Golf Association in earnings eight times and also served as president of the LPGA.

The first year they held it in Columbus, the Ladies' PGA was out at Walnut Hills Country Club. Kathy Whitworth had just won the LPGA championship and I had hoped to get an interview with her when she arrived for the tournament. Unfortunately, I was not able to be at the airport when she arrived and consequently was not able to set up a time to interview her before the 6 p.m. news that night.

I asked the tournament organizers who were meeting her at the airport if they would bring Kathy to the TV station so I could do a live interview. Kathy readily agreed and was there on time. She is typical of the gals on the LPGA tour. They appreciate media coverage and are willing to cooperate. I don't imagine you'd have found too many of the men who'd just won the PGA championship willing to come to a local TV station the next day to do an interview.

Kathy kidded me about the way I went about shooting my own film in those days. The Auricon sound camera I used was so noisy I couldn't get it close to where the golfers were.

To get some footage of Kathy at the tournament, I climbed through a trap door in the roof of the club house at Walnut Hills and shot my film from up there. Kathy looked up while she was playing and happened to spot me. She said she'd never seen anybody work as hard as I did to get pictures.

Kathy now appears only occasionally in tournaments. She announced her retirement in 1990 but, because of some bad investments, also let it be known that she can't afford to take it easy. She still plays in exhibitions and professional-amateur matches.

Kathy has always been well-liked and, as she's gotten older, has gotten the reputation of being a mother hen to the other golfers. In 1990, she was selected by her colleagues to captain the United States' first Solheim Cup team. As captain, she was an event manager rather than a player and did a great job of organizing. The U.S. team won and Kathy says she had the time of her life.

* * * *

Lee Trevino, who's now in his early fifties, is another golfer I'm proud to call a friend. Unlike a lot of golfers who come from privileged—or at least middle-class—backgrounds, Lee came from a poor home. He quit school at fourteen and worked at a country club to help support the family. His job gave him a close-up view of golf, a sport he perfected during two hitches in the special services unit of the Marines.

Lee's rise to affluence has not affected his wonderful personality and sense of humor. He has never been temperamental. In fact, he's been just the opposite and always has a joke or a stunt to delight his fans. The media come up with some pretty silly sports nicknames, and his fans are known as "Lee's fleas."

I remember being the brunt of one of his good-natured jokes on the first tee of the Muirfield Village Golf Club. I was covering a Pro-Am Day and was wearing a light-colored coat. Lee bellowed out as he walked up to me, "Well, I see you finally got a coat to match your hair." Of course, that drew a big laugh from the crowd.

But I got back at him a couple of years later. I had gotten a sports coat, probably the wildest I've ever worn, from LaVerne Hill, the widow of Charlie Hill, who had owned Scioto Downs. I was wearing it when Lee and I stood at the first tee, waiting for the Pro-Am to start.

As we chatted, a woman poked her hand through the ropes, tapped Lee's arm, and said, "Mr. Trevino, would you mind stepping aside while I get a picture of Jimmy Crum and his sports coat?" Trevino said, "Who in the hell is the star here, me or Crum?" He was kidding, of course, but I told him I felt I had gotten even!

All his joking around doesn't get in the way of Lee's playing. In 1968, only his second year on the PGA tour, he won the U.S. Open. Other golfers began to take him very seriously. In fact, Jack Nicklaus told him, "I hope you never find out how well you can play because it will give the rest of us a chance to win."

Lee won the Open again in 1971, after tossing a rubber snake at Jack on the first tee. That same year, Lee won the British Open, a win he repeated in 1972. In 1974 he won the PGA Championship.

Lee was out of commission for a couple of years in the mid-1970's while recuperating from being struck by lightning, and then from back surgery. He bounced back in 1979 and had one of best years of his career.

I'll always be grateful to Lee for giving me my first decent set of clubs. Years ago, Lee represented the Faultless Golf Company in Newark, Ohio. I got a call inviting me to do a story on the fact that he was going to be in Newark to inspect the line of clubs they manufacture. Faultless contacted several radio and TV stations, but I was the only person who showed up.

I followed Lee through the line as he inspected the Faultless equipment, then did an interview with him afterwards for Channel 4 News. When we were through, he asked if I played golf. I told him I did but that I'm a left-hander.

Lee turned to Joe Altamonte, the manufacturer's rep who was with us, and said, "Make Jim up a set of left-handed clubs at my expense and send them to him." I played with that set of clubs for many years, before switching to Altamonte's Pal Joey line of clubs.

Like Jack Nicklaus, Lee Trevino is now raising plenty of dust on the PGA Senior circuit. He's not yet ready to put away his clubs or his sense of humor, and the world is better for it.

* * * *

In terms of grit, determination, and working her way up from a tough life, Shirley Muldowney is a lot like Lee Trevino. Shirley has had a hard life, but you'd never know it from talking to her. She's a warm-hearted, caring type of person and has been a dear, sweet friend for many years. Known on the drag-racing circuit as "Cha Cha," Shirley dropped out of high school in 1956 at age fifteen to marry her first husband, a hot rodder named Jack Muldowney.

Shirley was always strong-minded and that's probably why she was able to talk her husband into letting her be the driver. If you saw the movie made about her life in 1983 called "Heart Like a Wheel," you know he was not what you'd call liberated. Neither were the racing officials, who were reluctant to let a woman race—especially a tiny, feminine-looking one like Shirley whose hands were perfectly manicured.

But Shirley was persistent and determined, and in 1973 became the first woman licensed as a top fuel driver by the National Hot Rod Association. She was severely burned in a horrible accident in a funny car that year. The accident nearly ended her career.

Shirley is not a quitter. She underwent plastic surgery and major rehabilitation and came back in 1976 to win a national championship race. Shirley drove top fuel dragsters, which accelerate from zero to 250 mph in six seconds. She won the NHRA championship three times—a first in drag racing history for any driver, male or female—and had 17 victories driving the top fuel cars.

In 1984, another horrible racing accident again nearly took her life. Shirley's legs were shattered and her pelvis was broken, but she underwent extensive physical therapy and again returned to racing.

Covering Shirley Muldowney and other racers has been one of the more exciting parts of my career. I covered my first Indy 500 race in 1946 and, with the exception of 1954 when I was on my honeymoon, covered every Indianapolis Motor Speedway race for the next 20 years until ABC began offering national coverage.

Using just one camera, I'd circle the two-and-a-half mile track to make it look like we had a number of different cameras on the race. Race officials were not as restrictive then about where photographers could go, and I'd get covered with grease and rubber dust from the race.

Getting that close to the action does carry risks, however, as I learned in 1958 when Ed Elesian's car went out of control and wiped out 14 other cars. One driver, Pat O'Connor, was killed when his car flipped end-over-end several times.

As I was filming this, a photographer from Channel 13 in Indianapolis suddenly grabbed me and pulled me back behind the retaining wall. A couple of seconds later, Jerry Unser's car—which had gone out of control—flew over our heads. I learned something important about safety from that incident. In the future, instead of closing one eye as I filmed, I kept both eyes open so I could see the approaching cars on the speedway.

* * * *

Jerry Unser's car was not my only near-miss on the racing circuit. Several years ago, George Follmer and Charlie Kemp were driving the two RC Cola Porsches in the Sports Car races at Mid-Ohio. George, a long-time friend, told me when they'd be testing and asked if I'd like to take a ride.

I said yes even before he finished asking the question. At that time, I was still shooting my own film for Channel 4, so I took my 16 mm camera with me and invited along a camera crew to take film of me filming the driver.

I rode with Charlie Kemp, who was helmeted, dressed in fire-retardant clothes, and strapped firmly into the driver's seat. I wore a helmet, a smile, and no belt because I was wedged into the tub next to the driver with one shoulder braced against his seat and the other against the car.

We took several laps at less than racing speed so I could get some good shots of Charlie's face, hands, and feet as he shifted gears and concentrated on the track. Then, when the signal was given, the car in front of us pulled aside and Charlie kicked in the afterburner. In a matter of seconds, we were traveling close to 180 miles an hour.

I quickly forgot about shooting film and tried to find a comfortable position. After about a dozen laps "at speed," Charlie pulled into the pits. My knees felt like jello, but I had experienced one of the greatest thrills ever.

The next day, when I was safely back in Columbus, Charlie took the car out again. On his second lap "at speed," the car's suspension broke as he headed into the first turn. The car flipped and landed on the inside grassy area of the track. The car was damaged but, fortunately, Charlie was not injured. It gave me pause, though! If that suspension had gone out a day earlier, this book might never have been written.

* * * *

No discussion of sports car racing friends would be complete without mentioning the 1986 Indy Champion, Bobby Rahal. Besides being a first-rate athlete, Bobby is a generous guy who served as honorary chairman of the Easter Seal Telethon for eight years. He's given us a lot of his time shooting publicity pictures with our Easter Seal child each year. His wife, Debi, has always been very involved, too.

Bobby has never fit the stereotype of the race car driver. In 1975, he was named top amateur driver by the Sports Car Club of America. What made the honor unusual was that he was a senior at Denison University at the time. After graduating with a degree in history, Bobby drove for three years in Formula Atlantic, then briefly worked for a Chicago advertising agency until 1981.

It was then that a family friend, the late Jim Trueman, founder of Red Roof Inns and president of TrueSports Racing, took Bobby under his wing and made him his driver. TrueSports quickly became one of the leaders on the Indy Car circuit.

In 1982, Bobby was named Championship Auto Racing Teams rookie of the year. Four years later, he won the Indianapolis 500, with an average speed of 170.7 miles per hour—the fastest in the history of the race. His final lap was also a record—he completed it in 43.031 seconds at a speed of 209.1 miles per hour. It was also the first year the race was broadcast live and it gave Bobby fantastic exposure.

A few days after the victory, Jim Trueman died of cancer. "In addition to giving a young driver a chance, Jim taught me about selflessness and commitment," Bobby said in tribute.

At Jim's funeral, his brother Jack shared this with me: "A group of his friends and family were talking the other night. We decided that three years ago when he learned he had cancer, Jim probably had a talk with God. God said to him, 'Jim, do you want to win the Indianapolis 500 or do you want to live a couple more years?' We figure that Jim's response was, 'Let me win the 500, God, and then we'll talk about it.'"

After Jim's death, Bobby left TrueSports to go with the Galles-Kraco race team based in Albuquerque. He stayed with Kraco for two years, and there was some disappointment on the part of Barbara Trueman, Jim's widow. In 1992 he established the Rahal-Hogan Miller Genuine Draft team and headquartered it in Indianapolis.

Later that year, Bobby brought his team back into the TrueSports' shop in Hilliard. It was a fantastic year for Miller and Hogan—one that far exceeded their wildest dreams and expectations. At year's end, Bobby once again captured the PPG Indy Car Drivers' Championship.

Another good thing that happened as a result of moving his operation back to town is that Bobby Rahal and Barbara Trueman have once again become the best of friends. As president of Red Roof Inns, she's one of the sponsors of the Rahal-Hogan Miller Genuine Draft team. It's great to see Bobby back here and it's also nice that he and Barbara have re-established their friendship.

* * * *

Another incredibly talented athlete—one who became like a second daughter to me—is diver Kelly McCormick, who won a silver medal in the 1984 Olympics and a bronze medal in 1988. Kelly is the daughter of Pat McCormick, who won double gold medals in platform and spring board diving in the 1952 and 1956 Olympics. You could say that talent runs in the family.

I had gotten to know Kelly through stories I'd done on her when she was on the Ohio State diving team. Both my wife, Miriam, and I got to know her well, and we fell in love with her spunk and spirit. Kelly's enthusiasm just sparkled, and in 1986 we decided at Channel 4 to do a long-running, two-year story on her preparation for the 1988 Olympic Games in Seoul, Korea.

During that time, every couple or three weeks I would update viewers on what she was doing in and out of the pool to prepare for the Olympics—from weight training to earning money to support her training as a part-time driver for Avis at Port Columbus.

A more exciting part of covering her preparation was a trip to Sydney, Australia, to cover Kelly and another Ohio State diver, Mary Ellen Clark, who were competing in an international meet. Kelly finished second to the brilliant Chinese diver, Gao Min, who later won the gold medal in the 1988 Olympic games. Kelly went on the win the bronze.

My photographer, Tim Moushey, and I followed Kelly wherever she went in Sydney—including to the city's world-famous zoo where officials rolled out the red carpet and gave us each a wombat to hold. Later, when Kelly landed a berth on the U.S. Olympic swim team after competing in the trials in Indianapolis, we put together a half-hour show called "Searching for Gold" that highlighted what we had done over those two years. I was very, very proud of the show and wanted to put it up for an Emmy.

Unfortunately, at that time we had a news director who did not believe in the Emmy competition and would not nominate the show—even though I had received an Emmy in 1977 on a documentary about the burn unit at Children's Hospital. To this day, I'm as proud of the program on Kelly as I am of the Children's Hospital documentary.

Over the years, Kelly, her mother, and I have kept in close touch. Every year, Pat comes back to Columbus to help with the Celebrity Waiters' Luncheon. In return, I go to California to play in Pat's golf tournament and act as master of ceremonies for the Pat McCormick Foundation's annual fundraiser to help get deserving kids through high school and into college.

Kelly, who retired from competitive diving after the 1988 Olympics, is married and on September 20, 1992, had a baby girl, Alexandra Patricia. I expect to see her, too, standing on the end of a diving board one of these days.

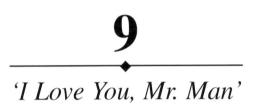

9

'I Love You, Mr. Man'

Ihave the reputation of being a reporter who calls them as he sees them. Because I do hang tough and say what I think, sports fans either love me or hate me. There doesn't seem to be any in-between. And that's fine with me because if you're getting no reactions in this business, you might as well pack it in and go home.

I know there have been better sportscasters in town, because they've left Columbus for larger, better-paying markets like Detroit, San Francisco and Los Angeles. I believe one of the things that's enabled me to last more than forty years in a profession where people are either fired or choose to move on, has been my involvement in community activities.

People associate that involvement with retarded and handicapped children—and rightly so—but I also have made a point of befriending children in general. I recently received a thank-you letter from Dave Tebay, whose son had met me at his preschool. An excerpt follows:

"I was pleasantly surprised last week when my four-year-old son, Brian, came home announcing that Jimmy Crum had visited his Dublin preschool. Brian went on to inform me that Jimmy Crum was on Channel

4 at 6 p.m. and that we need to watch Jimmy on television. I'm sure with your knowledge and experiences with children, you can appreciate my amazement that Brian had remembered, and absorbed that information to present to his dad. I know I have pointed him in the direction of being an OSU and Cincinnati Reds fan, but I didn't realize that he was also a Jimmy Crum fan."

When I began working with kids at Children's Hospital in 1955, two years after I started with Channel 4, I did so because I wanted to do something for the community in return for the nice life my family and I were enjoying in this town. I didn't realize at the time that my community involvement would eventually help give me credibility. I got involved simply because I wanted to. As Woody Hayes used to say, "You can never pay back, but you can pay forward." That's what I've tried to do.

Over the years I've participated as a volunteer and fund-raiser for many community organizations that help people of all ages, including those associated with sight saving, leukemia, cystic fibrosis, and the Kidney and Heart Foundations. But because of my special regard for children, the four I've been most closely associated with are Recreation Unlimited, Special Olympics, Easter Seals and the Burn Unit at Children's Hospital.

In almost forty years of befriending children, I have to say I've seen just as many—maybe even more—examples of courage among sick and disabled kids as I've seen on playing fields. Seeing hospitalized kids suffer took some getting used to. It was a phone call from the father of a boy named Mark Tate that got me involved with the Burn Unit at Children's.

A television antenna Mark and his father were erecting touched a high voltage wire, falling across Mark's body and severely injuring him. Among other injuries, Mark lost an arm—a particularly horrible thing to happen to a boy who loved to play baseball. Mark's father called me because Mark enjoyed seeing me cover sports on television and he thought I might be able to cheer up his son.

Unlike the doctors, nurses and physical therapists who had to cause him pain in order to treat him, I was someone who could talk and read to Mark and other patients—someone who cared but who was not directly involved in rehabilitation. My visits were not threatening and, because they'd seen me on TV, I was familiar to the children.

Burn treatment has come a long, long way in twenty years. In those days, what the kids went through was absolutely horrible. The physical therapist there often remarked that those kids thought of "PT," short for physical therapy, as "physical torture." Burn Unit patients like Mark Tate often stayed from three to six months, and I got to know these children quite well.

Because of the "magic" of television, my appearance at the hospital seemed magical as well. Thirty minutes after they'd seen me do a broadcast I'd often be in their rooms chatting with them. My only reason for being there was to put a smile on their faces—that's a goal of mine that hasn't changed a bit over the years.

Because of my connections with local sports figures, I was often able to get kids to grin from ear-to-ear by arranging visits from their idols. I remember my visits with two young hospitalized boys from the North Side of Columbus who had been in a house fire. One was very badly burned. The boy in the worst shape was absolutely gung-ho about Ohio State. The year was 1975 and he had pictures of Woody Hayes, Archie Griffin and Ohio Stadium up in his room at Children's.

Clearly, this thirteen-year-old boy was a fan, so I asked Woody to go with me after the 6 o'clock news one night. Woody readily agreed, but kept looking at his watch as we drove to the hospital. Finally he said, "I really should be looking at some films now for a meeting later. We'll just stay a minute, and you can bring me back for a longer visit some other time."

Right, Coach! Two hours later I dragged Woody from the boy's room. During the visit, the boy said how much he'd also like to meet Archie Griffin. Woody explained that Archie was so tied up with classes and football that he didn't know when he'd be able to find time to come to the hospital. As we left, the kid shook Woody's hand and said, "Coach, tell Archie I'll understand if he can't get out to see me."

That did it. The minute we walked out the door, Woody grabbed my lapels and ordered me to pick up Archie the following day. He'd make the arrangements with Archie. And naturally he did. Within 24 hours of saying he wanted to meet Archie Griffin, a very happy thirteen-year-old forgot his suffering as he chatted with his hero. Now that's magic!

In 1977, I wrote and produced a 30-minute documentary titled "Three

Tower North," on the mission of the doctors, nurses, and therapists at Children's Hospital Burn Unit. The program featured a little girl named Belinda Munday who had been badly burned in a fire in Parkersburg, West Virginia. She and some friends were who were helping her celebrate her eighth birthday carried candles into the barn behind Belinda's house. The hay inside the barn caught fire and Belinda and another girl were severely burned.

When Belinda arrived at Children's Burn Unit, she had second and third degree burns over forty-five percent of her body. She was a wonderful little girl, and very brave. While Belinda was recovering from her burns, I decided she'd be the ideal child to feature in a documentary, so we spent several weeks videotaping her and the medical personnel who played a part in her rehabilitation. Belinda had to re-learn many skills, including walking, and rehabilitation was excruciatingly painful for her.

The documentary included scenes with Dr. Tom Boles, chief of pediatric surgery, who had performed all the operations on Belinda, and Dawn Douce, head nurse on the Burn Unit. Dawn is an extremely caring and very articulate person, but on the morning of the taping she got a terrible case of nerves and told us she couldn't go through with the documentary.

My photographer was a very savvy guy named Bruce Johansson. As I tried to calm Dawn, I heard Bruce click on the video camera. I knew what he was up to, so I suggested to Dawn that we just do a dry run and rehearse the questions I planned to ask her.

Dawn relaxed, lit up her first in a chain of cigarettes, and began talking away. She did a beautiful job of answering my questions as she related stories about the tender loving care Belinda and other burn patients received. When she finished talking, I said, "Okay, we're through." I thought Dawn was going to have a heart attack when she found out we had been taping the actual interview!

We received a regional Emmy for "Three Tower North," which is where the Children's Hospital Burn Unit is located. I am more proud of that 1976 Emmy than anything else I've ever done. I won another in 1992 for a story I did on the TrueSport racing team called "Made in America." I won my third Emmy that same year, the Governor's Award from the National Academy of Arts and Sciences, for my service to the City of Columbus. But because Belinda Munday was such a wonderful little girl, the Emmy for "Three Tower North" still ranks first in my heart.

Over the years, I have kept in touch with Belinda and her family in Parkersburg. She and her mother come to Columbus during the Christmas holidays every year, and Miriam and I take them out to lunch. Belinda has had several major surgeries. She has some scar tissue but she walks fine, and it's always a special occasion when we see her.

I am sorry to say that not all my Children's Hospital stories have happy endings. One that broke my heart was the death of ten-year-old Jessica Stewart, who passed away in February, 1987. I first met Jessica, her twin, Jennifer, and their parents, Cindy and Bob Grewell, in the lobby of Children's Hospital. I had been at the hospital visiting other children and was on my way out when I saw two beautiful, healthy-looking, identical little blue-eyed blondes.

Jennifer was healthy, but a few days after our meeting, Jessica would check into Children's for a six-month stay. She had an inoperable tumor on her spine. Except for times when I was required to be out of town, I never missed a day of visiting her—Saturdays and Sundays included.

Shortly before she passed away, her mother told me Jessica had talked about her funeral. She'd asked what a eulogy was and Cindy had explained it was when somebody says something nice about you at your funeral. Jessica replied, "Mommy, I want Jimmy Crum to say something nice about me at my funeral."

Jessica died two weeks later, and I don't think I've faced a tougher situation in my life. During her six months on the unit, twenty-five nurses had cared for Jessica at one time or another. On the day of her funeral, they'd all managed to get other nurses to cover their shifts so they could be there for Jessica's family in Mount Sterling, where the service was held.

I have never seen such an outpouring of love and thoughtfulness as I witnessed at Jessica Stewart's funeral. It took me a while to get composed enough to deliver the eulogy that day, but somehow I got through it. Later, Cindy and Bob Grewell gave me an engraved plaque. It was a copy of the letter Jessica had dictated to her mother before she died.

"I love you guys a lot. And I just want to say, I can't wait until I see you guys up in heaven. I wanted this note read to my family and friends at my funeral so that everyone will know that I trust Jesus and I really am

sad and tired, but I'm not afraid and am ready to go to Him.
Love, Jessica"

There was not a dry eye in the house after Jessica's letter was read.

Jessica's family has stayed in close touch with my family. We have visited at their home in Mount Sterling many times. Cindy Grewell works in Grove City, and I sometimes drive down to take her to lunch.

Jennifer is happy and healthy. She got her driver's license and I've kidded her that I'm now steering clear of Mount Sterling. Every fall, I take a present to Jennifer on her birthday. Every February, I meet Cindy Grewell in Mount Sterling to put a rose on Jessica's grave.

Jessica can never be replaced. But her loss is in small measure balanced by special moments I have experienced with children who have not only survived, but triumphed. A special moment I will never forget occurred at one of our annual Easter Seal Telethons. Heather Boggs, who'd been our Easter Seal poster child three years earlier, made an appearance on the show to demonstrate the progress she'd made, thanks to the viewers who had supported her rehabilitation through Easter Seals.

Before bringing Heather on stage, we ran a videotape showing how she'd graduated from a walker to forearm crutches in the past three years. To my complete surprise, when the camera cut to Heather—who was several feet away from me on stage—she put down her crutches and walked very slowly into my arms.

Well, I just lost it at that point. I'd managed not to cry about the courage shown by Easter Seals kids during previous telethons. But Heather's walking was such a personal triumph for that little girl, I was moved to tears. So were the viewers. The phones rang off the hook.

When I got my composure back, I said, "Miracles really do happen. Here's a little girl who, three or four years ago, could not get around without a walker. You've just seen what they can do at the Easter Seal Rehab Center." Her mother later told me that Heather had practiced for six months for that courageous walk across the stage.

Thinking back to Heather's courage reminds me of the courage of another spunky kid, a fourteen-year-old named Julie Cochran. Julie was stricken with polio during the 1950's before the vaccines became available. The first time I saw her, Julie was encased in an iron lung at Children's Hospital. She was completely immobilized but she was determined that polio wasn't going to whip her. It didn't.

A year later when my wife and I visited her at home in Fredericktown, Ohio, Julie had progressed to a portable iron lung that covered her from her neck to her hips. Both Miriam and I fell in love with Julie. Her refusal to be beaten down by polio was absolutely awe-inspiring. Julie, who has remained a close friend, went on to become a speech therapist at Ohio State University.

When I met Julie in 1955, I was at Children's Hospital shooting film to show at halftime at the nationally-televised East-West Shrine game, an annual charity event to raise money for polio victims. The Shriners' fundraising slogan was "Strong legs run so weak legs may walk." Woody Hayes was coaching the East Team, which included some Buckeyes, at Kezar Stadium in San Francisco where the game was held. Jim Rhodes, who was then city auditor, Dr. Jud Wilson, who was head of orthopedics at Children's Hospital, and I devised a fundraiser to capitalize on the Buckeyes' participation in the game.

During half time, I showed the film I had taken at Children's Hospital to local viewers and explained the purpose of the fund we'd established. We called it "Bucks for Braces"—referring to leg braces worn by polio victims—and asked viewers to send in a buck each to help treat children suffering from the disease. The response was tremendous, just as the response in Columbus has been to Recreation Unlimited.

Because I've been associated with Recreation Unlimited for more than twenty-five years, many people erroneously assume that it was my brainchild. In fact, the idea for a camp for the mentally and physically handicapped came about back in 1957 as a result of the dedication of a man named Dick Ruff. Dick was born without a complete set of limbs—one hand was missing and his other arm ended at the elbow. One leg ended at the hip. The foot on the other leg was half-size.

Thanks to parents who accepted, loved and encouraged him, Dick found ways to master the physical skills necessary to become self-sufficient. He attended regular public schools in Cleveland—this was back in the 1940's before "mainstreaming" was a trend—where he used his fine mind and his fighting spirit to overcome what others might have accepted as limitations. If Dick had been content with ordinary goals, he would have become a scholar—certainly a very worthwhile ambition.

Instead, despite the odds, he developed his athletic as well as his mental abilities. Dick was a golfer, a bowler and a softball pitcher. He was a high jumper at Rhodes High School in Cleveland. He also was a place-kicker for the Rhodes High football team. Dick told me he often kidded his coach by saying, "You don't have to worry about a penalty for holding being called on me, coach, 'cause I've got nothing to hold on with!"

Another of his favorite jokes was, "I can do anything other people can do, except tie my own shoes. That's why I wear loafers." Clearly, Dick didn't spend much time feeling sorry for himself. Because his attitude was so positive, it was impossible for those who knew him to pity him. That suited Dick just fine. It was this refusal to view himself as different that most impressed me when I met Dick back in 1959. At that time he was a social worker at the old Ohio State School for the Handicapped and Retarded in Columbus.

With the help of Columbus businessmen Wilmore Brown and William Mitchell, Dick had been raising money to send handicapped and retarded kids to camps around Ohio during the weeks when other kids' groups weren't using them. Despite their best efforts, they were nearly two thousand dollars in debt and camps were refusing to extend credit.

Dick called me because he thought I might be able to get Channel 4 involved with the fundraising. It was a smart move on his part, because in order for Recreation Unlimited to survive, Dick was going to need public support.

After talking with Dick, I came away fired up about the idea and went straight to Walter Bartlett, who was then our station manager. Walter thought the station could help and, along with reporter Dave Collins and I, set up the TV 4 Sports Fund to raise money for Recreation Unlimited. We chartered both organizations through the State Attorney General's Office as nonprofit charities.

In 1965, the first year we appealed to viewers, we raised forty-seven hundred dollars—enough to pay off debts and send four dozen children to camp for one week. Dick, Dave, Walter and I were all flying! We were just astounded at the generous response from viewers. Last year, we raised more than eight hundred and sixty thousand dollars.

One of our most long-term and successful fundraisers has been the annual Celebrity Waiters' Luncheon, which was first held in 1971. My idea was to have local celebrities wait tables (with a lot of help from experienced staff!), with the tips they collected going to Recreation Unlimited. Woody Hayes, John Glenn, John W. Galbreath, Bill Hoskett and Randy Gradishar helped me wait tables that first year. Together, we raised about a thousand dollars.

Except for a couple of years in the late seventies when bad weather and my overburdened scheduled prevented me from organizing the event, Celebrity Waiters has been a fine annual fundraiser and a lot of fun. Word of its success has gotten out, and I've traveled to several cities to show others how to organize and run this type of fundraiser.

Karen Benningfield, who I worked with at Easter Seals, deserves most of the credit for its continuing success in Columbus. She got involved in 1980 and began enlisting corporate sponsors. She has done a great job of managing the whole event. Last year, we raised $130,000 from corporations and small donors.

The diversity of contributors to the Celebrity Waiters' Luncheon is typical of the growth in the number and type of donors we've seen in all our fundraising activities. We have moved from individual donors responding to Channel 4's simple on-air request, to having a number of major donors—as well as a very necessary army of small donors, all responding generously to a variety of fundraising efforts.

Some of my personal fundraising efforts have been very direct. In 1988, I saw some pontoon boats on an RV lot owned by Steve Cross near Alum Creek reservoir. When I asked him about a giving Recreation Unlimited a special rental rate, Steve promptly obliged. The following year, he built a special handicap-accessible pontoon boat and gave it to Recreation Unlimited. He has since visited the camp several times to take the kids out on the boat to fish.

Our major donors include Larry Liebert, who is also chairman of Recreation Unlimited; the late Jim Trueman, CEO of Red Roof Inns; Dave Thomas of Wendy's; pro golfer and businessman, Jack Nicklaus, and so many others that it would take pages to list.

Special thanks go to Dave Thomas, who gave Recreation Unlimited an interest-free loan so we could buy the property in 1983. In 1987, at a dinner following the annual Dave Thomas Invitational Golf Tournament for Recreation Unlimited, Dave raised nearly $900,000 in pledges from tournament players. It stands as the biggest-ever single-night fundraiser in our history.

It's because of the generosity of these and hundreds of other donors that, after many years of sending children to other camps, Recreation Unlimited in 1989 opened its own 160-acre site on Piper Road in northeast Delaware County.

The property is beautiful. It includes ponds, open fields and woods, and is home to geese and other wildlife. Indoors and out, it's designed to facilitate independence among our retarded and handicapped campers.

Recreation Unlimited facilities aren't meant for any one particular group of handicapped people. Space permitting, all handicapped campers are welcome. So that staff can be available to meet various needs, campers come for a week at a time in three different categories: physically handicapped campers, mentally handicapped campers, and multi-handicapped campers.

Computer people talk about making their machines "user-friendly." Well, we've worked hard to make our site "camper-friendly." We've leveled, widened and blacktopped our walking trails, for instance, so that they can be used by those in wheelchairs. We've recruited camp counselors from all over Ohio who are experienced in working with retarded and handicapped children. And we're staffed with an extremely high ratio of counselors to campers, so that campers get the unobtrusive help they need to participate as fully as possible.

When you hear me talk about Recreation Unlimited on TV, there is more to the name than just the initials RU. Through Ohio's nonprofit Charitable Solicitations Board, Recreation Unlimited is known officially as "Recreation Unlimited Farm and Fun, Inc." The initials spell the last name of its founder, Dick Ruff, who thirty years ago dreamed of having a camp for people with disabilities. Those of us connected with Recreation Unlimited are now living out his dream.

Meeting Recreation Unlimited campers has been an eye-opener for many of the people involved with creating the camp, most of whom haven't spent much time with retarded and handicapped people. The experience of Kent Brandt, one of the architects for the camp, was typical.

After working with us for several months on the camp's concept and design, Kent went with me one day to Camp Ohio, a 4-H site in Licking

County we'd been using for several years. A camper named Tommy Noble came over to chat with us. During the conversation, I asked Tommy what he'd been doing since last summer.

His response: "Waiting to come back to camp this year!" Kent told me later that it at that moment that he truly understood what Recreation Unlimited was all about.

Because I work with so many organizations, I often see our campers other places as well. Lisa Amos, for example, has won a silver medal in diving in international competition in Special Olympics. Lisa has Down's Syndrome and it's frightening to realize that only a generation ago, expectations for her would have been about zero.

Many of the children I meet through Easter Seals and other organizations also become Recreation Unlimited campers if they meet our age requirement. Campers must be at least eight years old, but there's no cap at the other end—we have some campers in their sixties who have every bit as much fun as the kids.

Recreation Unlimited's camp director, David Hoy, puts it very well in the orientation and welcome speech he makes each year to our counselors. David always begins by asking the staff, "Is there anyone here who is perfect?" Of course, no one ever raises a hand. He then emphasizes that counselors are to focus on the similarities between themselves and campers instead of on the differences.

The general public has also become much more sensitive to the fact that handicapped and retarded children need opportunities to develop their physical and mental skills to the best of their abilities. These kids don't want to be pitied. Like you and I, they want to respect themselves and to have others respect them. And, given the chance, most will do their darndest to succeed.

I will never forget going to a bowling tournament for several dozen handicapped and retarded children held at Western Lanes 30 years ago. I knew other media would not find the event newsworthy, so I went to cover it as a human interest story.

As I was shooting film, I noticed a tiny girl over on lane number one who was pushing and shoving a bowling ball down the alley. She was so small that every ball she bowled was a gutter ball, yet she used fantastic body English to try to influence the ball's direction. The little girl was so determined that I decided I had to shoot close-ups of her. When I approached the girl, I saw she had Down's Syndrome and she was just as cute as she could be.

I photographed her as she pushed a ball right down the center of the lane. She had been happy before, but now she was ecstatic. After capturing her moment of triumph on film, I put down my camera and went over and knelt beside her.

"You sure are a good bowler," I told her. She'd never laid eyes on me before, but the minute the words were out of my mouth, this little girl wrapped her arms around my neck and gave me a big hug. Then she put her face next to mine and whispered, "I love you, Mr. Man."

I spent the rest of the afternoon wiping my eyes. When people ask me what I get in return for all the time I've spent with kids, I answer honestly, "They give me one hell of a lot more than I could ever give them."

10

The 19th Hole

The 19th hole, as any golfer knows, is that extra hole where golfers—win, lose, or draw—sit down and tell about the putts that could have been and the putts that should have been. It's the place where a 20-foot putt for an eagle on number seven all of a sudden becomes a 30-foot putt. It's the place to talk about sports and sportsmanship, and friends in general, and that's what this chapter is all about.

* * * *

In 1984, I received the Sertoma International Service to Mankind Award in Toronto, Canada. It led to a meeting with President Reagan in the Oval Office, which was one of the proudest moments of my life.

As it turned out, President Reagan's schedule was extremely busy, and it was nearly a year before the customary meeting with the award recipient could be arranged. Congressman John Kasich was the real mover behind getting the meeting set up; I had put my hopes of it happening so far on the back burner that I had nearly forgotten about it.

The news that I would actually get to meet Mr. Reagan came toward the end of a very busy day. I'd gotten up at 4 a.m. to drive to Athens, Ohio, to play in a charity golf tournament, and then raced back here to meet at my home that afternoon with Channel 4's "PM Magazine" hosts Lee Jordon and John Huffman. They were going to emcee a telethon and wanted some advice from me how to go about it.

When they arrived for our meeting, Lee Jordan immediately asked if I had called in to the station that day. When I told her I had been too busy to do so, she said I should call right away to get the message left by President Reagan's office. Lee eventually convinced me she wasn't kidding, so I called the station and got the number that had been left for me—that of President Reagan's appointment secretary. I called Washington at about 3:30 p.m. on a Friday afternoon and was told the President could meet with me the following Monday afternoon at 4 p.m.

Naturally, I was on cloud nine. My wife, Miriam, was also very excited. She went out the next morning and bought a red-trimmed dress, red shoes, and a red purse because it was known that President Reagan liked red.

We flew to Washington two days later on a Monday morning and had lunch with Congressman John Kasich and members of his staff. After lunch, we went to the White House, arriving at 3:30 p.m. to allow time to be cleared through security at the front gate. The security folks had done all their homework. They had our social security numbers and other identifying information, and the guards let us through after we showed our drivers' licenses.

After passing through the gate, the first thing we saw was a Marine sergeant standing at the entrance to the White House. He snapped to attention and gave me a sharp salute when he opened the door for us. I had been an enlisted man in the Marine Corps in World War II, and his salute gave me quite a thrill.

We were then directed to a waiting room, where we sat until we were called to meet the President. A few minutes after we sat down, we were joined by Armand Hammer, who told us he had a 4:20 p.m. appointment with Mr. Reagan.

Miriam and I chatted with Mr. Hammer until Congressman Kasich and a liaison officer arrived to show us the cabinet room where the President meets with his advisors. I noticed a cube on the table in front of

President Reagan's chair and the liaison man told me I could examine it.

When I picked it up, I saw the word YES on one side, and on the opposite side, the word NO. On the other two sides were the phrases I DON'T KNOW and WHO CARES? We all got a big chuckle out of imagining the President using that cube during cabinet meetings.

Finally, we were ushered down a hallway to the Oval Office. Flanking the door were two huge Secret Service men wearing ear sets and listening to who knows what instructions. They opened the door for us, and standing by his desk was President Reagan.

I do not usually get stage fright, but when I saw the President of the United States, my heart began hammering about a hundred miles a minute. President Reagan is an extremely gracious man, and he immediately put us at ease. He commended me for my work with retarded and handicapped citizens, and then asked about Woody Hayes, who had recently suffered a heart attack.

We chatted about the President's sportscasting days in Des Moines, Iowa—when he was known as "Dutch" Reagan—and about sports in general. The President then described a day in 1935 when he was broadcasting a game between the University of Iowa and Drake. On that same day, he recalled, Ohio State played Notre Dame at Ohio Stadium.

During the broadcast, he learned via a Western Union ticker tape that Ohio State had lost to Notre Dame following a touchdown pass by a Notre Dame player named William Shakespeare. President Reagan said he had his people in the broadcast room check with Western Union on the score because he couldn't believe Ohio State had lost.

As we ended our chat, President Reagan presented Miriam with a stick pin with the Presidential seal on the front and his signature on the back. He then gave me a pair of cufflinks with the seal and his signature. I gave the President an Ohio State football jersey with his name and the number 1 on it. Then Miriam and I shook hands with him again before being escorted out of the office by the two burly Secret Service agents.

* * * *

The Sertoma award that led to my meeting with President Reagan was presented in Toronto, Canada, on June 16, 1984. When I flew to Toronto to receive it, Channel 4 sent along some videotape so I could get one of the stations there to record the event for our local news.

I carried the videotape instead of packing it to keep it from possibly being damaged by the airport's metal detector security devices. There was no problem with this in Columbus, but when I went through Canadian customs I got into some difficulty because I had forgotten to declare the videotape on the customs sheet provided on the airplane. The customs official asked if the blank videotape was something that could be sold in Canada, and I had to honestly answer yes.

As my fellow passengers breezed through customs, I got sent to another line to explain why I was carrying the videotape. I told the official I'd brought it along to record the award I was to receive, and was obliged to explain in great detail about why I was getting the award and why videotaping it was a good idea. After ten minutes, the customs agent shook my hand, said "Congratulations!" and welcomed me to Canada.

I was finally allowed to join my wife, who—like everyone else on the plane—had gone through customs without a snag. As we walked through the Toronto airport, a huge, bald man who looked like Attila the Hun approached us. He flashed a marshal's badge, then grabbed my arm and said, "Mr. Crum, you're under arrest."

First I'd had to go through the big deal over the videotape, and now this gargantuan Mr. Clean was strong-arming me. I felt such panic that I could hardly speak. I was about ready to fly home and change my underwear—that's how scared I was. Finally, I managed to squeak out, "Why am I being arrested?"

The man gave me a stern look, then bent down and whispered, "For wearing such a ##!#!! lousy sports coat into our great country of Canada."

I heard a group of guys cracking up nearby and was told that all of them, including Attila, were local Sertoma Club members. They'd cooked up this little stunt with the Ohio Sertoma Club that had nominated me for the award. I had a good laugh over the whole episode, and we all told the false arrest story many times during the five days I was at the Sertoma International convention.

* * * *

The "arrest" in Canada happened a few years after some real trouble with the FBI in Columbus. The incident occurred in 1979, just prior to the

Easter Seal Telethon. I'd gone to Florida for a vacation and, upon my return, was told by a porter at the Columbus airport, "Jimmy, the FBI is after you."

As I later learned, the Easter Seal Society had publicized the upcoming telethon by printing 50,000 handbills with the date of the telethon, along with my picture and that of the 1979 Easter Seal poster child. The design and printing were so good that U.S. Treasury agents said the bills looked like counterfeit money. The Secret Service was directed to confiscate them.

Garry Jenkins, the special agent in charge of recovering the bills, told me, "We're not too proud of what we have to do—it's like being against motherhood. But Easter Seal did violate the law."

The story was in the papers and on TV, and turned out to be the best free publicity we ever had for a telethon.

* * * *

In 1954, I was invited to appear on the "Today Show" with Dave Garroway to talk about Big Ten football. A sports reporter from each of the Big Ten cities was selected, and since Channel 4 was the NBC affiliate, I was the natural choice.

NBC flew me into New York City the night before the show and put me up in a nice hotel. The next morning, they sent a limousine to pick me up at 4:30 a.m. and take me to the studio.

In those days, everything on TV was live. When I arrived, Dave Garroway, Jack Lescoulie and Frank Blair were rehearsing their commercials and getting prepared to go on the air at 7 a.m. At 6:58 a.m., for no apparent reason, Dave Garroway collapsed. I watched as he was put on a stretcher and carried out of the studio.

Precisely at 7 a.m., Jack Lescoulie stepped before the cameras and said, " Good morning, everybody. This is the 'Today Show' from NBC. Dave Garroway is not feeling well this morning, and I'm Jack Lescoulie. Along with Frank Blair, I'll be here for the next two hours."

At that point, no one knew whether Dave Garroway was dead or alive. Yet Jack Lescoulie turned in one of the greatest performances I had ever seen, and chatted with the guests as though nothing was wrong. After the show we learned Dave Garroway had collapsed from exhaustion. He returned to the show two days later.

Needless to say, seeing the star of the show being carted off didn't do much for my confidence level—which at 26, was not too high to begin with. I felt very nervous as I stood in the wings, waiting to go on national TV and discuss OSU football. My anxiety was allayed by the beautiful Polly Bergen, a regular on the show, who chatted with me before I went on the air. She undoubtedly noticed my nervousness. When I told her what I did for a living, she put me at ease by gazing at me with those beautiful eyes and murmuring, "I've never met a real sportscaster before."

Her comment made me feel about ten feet tall.

* * * *

One of my very best friends is Dave Thomas, who's been a great supporter of Recreation Unlimited, as well as a philanthropist for a number of other charities. Dave and I met back in the early 1960's when he came to Columbus to work for Kentucky Fried Chicken.

Dave had become friends with several Baltimore Colts football players, including Gino Marchetti, an all-pro defensive end, and Alan Ameche. Ameche, a fullback, had played against Ohio State when he was at the University of Wisconsin. He was quite a powerful college player, and Woody Hayes used to say, "Alan Ameche always killed everybody else in the Big Ten, but he never hurt Ohio State."

In their day, these guys were as famous as Joe Montana is now, and Dave used to periodically bring them to town to make personal appearances at his restaurant. He'd call me up and offer me an exclusive interview with them, which of course I jumped at.

There was a catch to it, though. Dave would always add, "Remember, Jim, you've got to interview them out front, so viewers can see my Kentucky Fried Chicken sign."

* * * *

Another good friend of mine is Billy Maxted, who is now semi-retired and living in Ft. Lauderdale, Florida. Back in the 1950's, he had a great jazz band called Billy Maxted's Manhattan Jazz Band. He often played in Columbus at the old Grandview Inn when he was not performing at Nick's in Greenwich Village.

Over the years, Miriam and I became close friends with Billy and his wife, Inez. I'm convinced that one reason my daughter, Kelly, who's recognized as one of Columbus' top jazz singers, is so talented is that Miriam and I spent many nights listening to Billy and his band perform while Miriam was carrying her.

When Kelly was born in September of 1957, my first call was not to my parents or Miriam's, but to Nick's in Greenwich Village to let Billy Maxted know my daughter had arrived.

* * * *

I first met Arnold Schwarzenegger back in the 1970's when Jim Lorimer, who at that time was mayor of Worthington and an executive at Nationwide Insurance, promoted the Mr. Universe contest here in Columbus. From the start, the contest attracted top bodybuilders, and at that time Arnold was the number one body builder in the world.

On Arnold's first visit to Columbus, he held a press conference at Victoria's Station, a restaurant up on Route 161 that has since closed. When I did that first interview with Arnold, his English was not very good—he's a native of Austria—but his enthusiasm and sincerity rang out loud and clear. We established a friendship right away, and it has continued over the years.

After he and Maria were married, I told him, "Arnold, you're a lucky guy to be married to this beautiful lady, but she kissed me before she kissed you!" It had happened years before when I received an award from the Kennedy Foundation for Special Olympics for a program we had done on the Ohio Special Olympics.

The award was presented at a ceremony in Atlanta by Maria Shriver, who kissed me when she made the presentation. I had known her mother, Eunice Kennedy Shriver, because of my work as founding chairman of the Ohio Special Olympics, and got to know Maria, too. Arnold got a big kick out the fact that I had met—and kissed—Maria before he did.

Arnold has a great sense of humor and the man is no phony—what you see is what you get. He is also a man who keeps his word. For the past five years his Arnold Schwarzenegger Body Building Classic has overlapped with the Easter Seal Telethon. Except for 1993, when he was unable to make it because of a scheduling conflict, Arnold has always come out to the telethon and answered phones. Maria comes along, too, if she's traveling with him. This year, he called me from Port Columbus. He was on his way to New York in his private jet, and we did a live telephone interview.

"Jim," he said, as we wound up our interview, "I apologize for not being there. To make up for it, I'm pledging $5,000 to your Easter Seal Telethon." Just as he had promised, a week later the Easter Seal office received Arnold's $5,000 check.

* * * *

Two of the best basketball officials I ever knew were Jim Enright, who was also a sportswriter for one of the Chicago papers, and Lennie Wirtz, from Cincinnati. Jim, who has passed away, was in great demand and officiated at many NCAA championship games.

Lennie Wirtz is still at it today, fifty years after beginning his career officiating in the Big Ten. Lennie was the kind of official a crowd respected; everyone shut up to listen to his calls. He was fair and, more important, he actually admitted it when he made a mistake.

One night at a Minnesota-Wisconsin game, there was a foul called at one end of the floor. There's an old saying in basketball, "No harm—no foul," so Lennie let play continue without calling a foul.

Thirty seconds later at the other end of the floor, something almost identical happened and, without thinking, Lennie blew his whistle to signify a foul. He realized immediately what he'd done and, instead of letting it go as most officials would have, he shouted as loud as he could: "I blew it!"

That shows why Lennie Wirtz, who's now officiating at Atlanta Coast Conference games, is still so well-respected today.

* * * *

On a sports scale of 1 to 10, I would rank John Havlicek a 9.9—but only because nobody's perfect. Joining him in that 9.9 ranking would be Jack Nicklaus, Archie Griffin, Hop Cassady, Jim Parker, Vic Janowicz, Jerry Lucas, Jesse Owens, Bobby Rahal, Woody Hayes, Fred Taylor, and Randy Ayers, just to name a few.

These near-perfect rankings of mine are based on a number of things I've observed about these guys: their competitiveness, desire, determination, physical ability, and mental approach, to name just a few.

John Havlicek—or "Hondo," as he's known to many people—tops the list. During pre-season drills in 1962 when he was Ohio State's basketball captain, Hondo and his teammates trained by running up the steps in Ohio Stadium wearing ankle weights.

Once when he was taking a break from the steps, the football team was coming onto the field and Hondo decided to do some throwing with football player Tom Matte, who later had a distinguished career with the Baltimore Colts. Hondo took the football from Matte and said, "Fade back and I'll throw you one."

Hondo was standing at the goal line on the south end of the stadium, so Matte went back to about the 30 yard line. Hondo told Matte to go deeper, so Tom went back to the 50. Hondo wound up and threw it a good 65 yards, over Matte's head, then turned to Kaye Kessler and me and said simply, "My arm's a little bit sore. I can throw deeper than that."

John Havlicek wasn't bragging. That has never been his style. Hondo had been an excellent high school football player, and he was just stating a fact. When he graduated from Ohio State, Paul Brown, who was then coaching the Cleveland Browns, made him his seventh-round draft choice. Havlicek, of course, did not make the team. Instead, he became one of the all-time greats in the NBA. But Paul Brown told me later that if he'd had the luxury of keeping another player to bring along slowly for an NFL career, it would have been John Havlicek.

Later, when he received a $5,000 award for Rookie of the Year on a live TV broadcast, he thanked the sponsors, and gave half the money to a charity in Boston. Then he said, "I want to give the other $2,500 to Jimmy Crum for his Recreation Unlimited camp in Columbus, Ohio." I was watching the broadcast at Channel 4 and, needless to say, I was very surprised and deeply touched.

* * * *

After John Havlicek graduated, we did an hour documentary on the team's three years of greatness. They'd won the NCAA championship in 1960, and finished second to Cincinnati in 1961 and 1962. Novice Fawcett was president of Ohio State at the time, and I interviewed him for his opinion of the team's success. Dr. Fawcett, an eloquent speaker, had a magnificent command of the language. I'm paraphrasing what he said:

"The thing that has impressed me about these players [center John Havlicek, forwards Jerry Lucas and Joe Roberts, and guards Larry Sigfried, and Mel Nowell] is not what they did in victory, but the way they handled themselves in defeat. It would have been easy for them, after winning the national championship in 1960, to fold after losing to Cincinnati in 1961 and 1962. But they showed more character in losing than in winning. There are going to be times after they leave the university when they suffer losses and setbacks. But they've proved to me that they can handle adversity. And that's the best lesson they could have learned."

* * * *

Back when I was doing Ohio State football for WRFD Radio in 1951 and 1952, I did something that—had it been known at the time—probably would have gotten me and the station kicked out of broadcasting. The radio station's general manager was Joe Bradshaw, and the studios were located on the second and third floors of the Worthington Inn.

We discovered a week or so before the Michigan-Ohio State game that our request for credentials to cover the game had arrived too late, and there was no broadcasting space for WRFD at Michigan Stadium. This put us in quite a dilemma, because we were sponsored by the Farm Bureau and Nationwide Insurance, and the station had to broadcast that OSU-Michigan game to fulfill our contract with them.

So this is what we did: Dave Collins and I sat on the second floor at WRFD in the Worthington Inn watching a television broadcast of the game and reporting it on radio as though we were live in Ann Arbor. Needless to say, it was one of the most difficult games I have ever broadcast. If the TV cameras didn't show a wide shot of the field, it was hard to figure out exactly what yard line the ball was on. And if Joe Hill, the TV commentator, didn't say something specifically about where the ball was in play, Dave Collins and I had to try and guess where the ball was. But we got through it and, until now, nobody ever found out.

* * * *

Back in 1959, WCMH became the first station to televise Ohio State basketball. As every basketball fan knows, 1959-60 was the year Ohio State won the NCAA championship.

We did not have a production manager at Channel 4 then, so the station's program director told me to call all the Big Ten schools and see what it would cost us in rights fees to televise from each of the schools. Today, that figure is in the thousands and thousands of dollars. Back then, we had no idea what it might be.

I called nine of the schools and got quotes ranging from two hundred to five hundred dollars—the highest being Michigan. The last school I happened to call was Northwestern, whose sports information director was Walt Paulison.

Walt was an older guy and a legendary figure in the Big Ten. He was very well-respected, and had a distinctive, hesitant way of speaking. When I asked Walt what the rights fees would be to televise from Northwestern, he said, "Well, I, uh, well, we've never done this before and, uh, would twenty-five bucks be too much?"

That's probably the best deal the station ever got.

* * * *

Another story from those early days occurred back in the 1960's before Phil Donahue became a nationally syndicated talk show host. Donahue was doing his show locally at WLW-D in Dayton every morning and I was there, as AFTRA president, to negotiate a union contract for my colleagues at WLW-D.

The meeting had begun at 8 a.m. and we had been going hot and heavy for an hour. Those negotiating sessions sometimes got very tense and we were all at the breaking point when we learned Donahue was having a very special guest on his show. Promptly at 9 a.m., we set aside our animosities and together rushed to the studio window to look at Jayne Mansfield.

* * * *

I had the dubious distinction of being called on the carpet by Muhammad Ali when he was world heavyweight boxing champion. Incidentally, Ali's career record of 56-5 includes 37 knockouts.

What knocked me out about Ali, though, was what I observed about his patience and sense of humor when he visited Columbus to pick up a custom-designed motor coach from Kirwin Elmer and Buddy Byers. Byers, a college fraternity brother of mine and president of Byers Chrysler Plymouth, called me at the TV station to invite me over to interview Ali.

I took along a photographer from the station who, as soon as we got there, began to have trouble with his equipment. It ended up taking 45 minutes to do a two-minute interview with Ali. Ali was very gracious to me while the photographer fooled around with the equipment. He showed me through the coach and chatted away.

Finally, we were set to film the interview, and I did the 3-2-1 countdown as I always do right as we roll the film. Before I got a chance to ask a single question, though, Muhammad Ali jumped in and said:

"I like your class.

I like your style.

But your equipment's so bad,

I won't come back for a while."

Well, needless to say, it broke everybody up and we went on to have a good interview. I later showed the tape to our general manager and said, "This is what the world heavyweight champion thinks of our equipment." I'm not sure it helped, but shortly thereafter we did get some new photographic equipment.

* * * *

In 1966, Channel 4 did a 13-week series called "Echoes of Scarlet and Gray." My co-host for the series was the late Ernie Godfrey, longtime assistant Ohio State football coach. In each of the pre-taped, one-hour shows, Ernie and I focused on one of the top thirteen Ohio State football seasons between 1935 and 1965. We ran film clips of various games, and interviewed coaches and players about their recollections of each season's high and low points.

Since many of the former Ohio State players were still active in the National Football League, it wasn't possible for them to come to Columbus for the interviews. I decided to go to them. TWA and I worked together for several weeks to come up with an incredibly strenuous schedule that allowed me to talk with players in six NFL cities in one day.

On the appointed day, I took off from Columbus at 7 a.m. with a big Auricon sound camera over my shoulder. On my lap was a changing bag that I used to change film in the camera without exposing it to light. My first stop was Baltimore, where three members of the Colts team—Tom Matte, Bob Voegel and Jim Parker—met me at the airport. TWA had arranged for us to use a VIP room for the interviews; we did our thing, then I ran off to catch another plane.

Next stop: New York City, where Jets' fullback Matt Snell met me and I again conducted an interview in an airport VIP room. Then it was back to gate H-27 to depart for Cleveland, where I met with Paul Warfield, Dick Schafrath and Jim Houston. Same schtick, then back to another plane and another city—Detroit.

In the Detroit airport I interviewed Dick LeBeau, who later became defensive coordinator for the Cincinnati Bengals. Then I was back in the air to Kansas City for an airport conversation with Jim Tyrer, a Newark, Ohio, native who had been the OSU football team's co-captain in 1960.

The final leg of the one-day flight took me to Minneapolis. I arrived just before midnight and was met at the airport by Minnesota Vikings' tackle Jim Marshall. And guess what? I was out of film. Fortunately, Jim worked for a Minneapolis TV station.

We drove to his station, where he gave me some film, and we did the interview about 1 a.m. My day, which had started 18 hours before in Columbus, was finally over. I checked into a hotel and got a few hours of sleep before heading back home. It had been a grueling day and night, but it was worth it—in one fell swoop I had assembled plenty of great interviews to spice up the 13-week series.

* * * *

One of the shows in the 1966 series, "Echoes of Scarlet and Gray," focused on Ohio State's 1941 team. The captain of that team, Jack Stevenson, joined Ernie Godfrey and me on the show to talk about the season and his experiences with Paul Brown, when Brown was in his first year as Ohio State's head football coach.

Jack was a big man for his time—about 6'4" or 6'5"—and had been a great tackle for Ohio State. But he told us he had been scared to death of Paul Brown, a much smaller man.

Brown's reputation from Massillon High School, where he'd been a stern coach, had preceded him. Adding to Jack's fear was the rumor that the season opener against Missouri was going to feature something brand new and top secret. It turned out to be the split T formation, developed by Missouri coach Don Farout.

As Jack tells it, before that Missouri game the team had assembled inside the tunnel in the southeast corner of Ohio Stadium, where they waited for the official to come over and get the captain for the coin toss. Jack, who was a good eight inches taller than Paul Brown, looked out the door and saw the American flag standing straight out, indicating a strong wind from the south.

Jack tapped his coach's arm and, in a friendly way, said, "Coach, I think we should take the wind at our backs the first quarter and shove the ball right down their throats."

Jack said Brown reached up and grabbed him by the shoulder pads, spun him around, and in a voice that everyone in the tunnel could hear, responded: "Mr. Stevenson, don't you ever think again! I'll think for this team."

If there was any doubt as to who was in charge, Jack said Paul Brown's comment made it clear. By the way, despite the split-T, OSU won the ball game 12-7. Several years later, when I was broadcasting the Bengals' games on the Bengals Radio Network, I related Jack's story to Paul Brown, who was then coaching the Bengals, and asked if it was true. He just smiled and said, "It was something like that."

* * * *

Speaking of Paul Brown, he was not one of those guys who mellowed out as he got older. Several years ago, when he was in his late sixties or early seventies, he was elected to the Ohio Senior Citzens Hall of Fame. A few years previously, his first wife, Katie, had passed away and he had married his secretary, Mary. She was quite a bit younger than Paul, and he did not take kindly to being classified as a senior citizen.

Maybe that's why he asked me to accept his plaque for him at the Martin Janis Senior Citizen Center on the Ohio State fairgrounds. I was doing the Bengals' games on the Bengals' Radio Network, and said I would go on his behalf. I was very glad I did. There were half a dozen other Ohio-born senior citizens being honored that day, and I got to sit on stage between two of them. On one side was Phyllis Diller. On the other was Lillian Gish.

* * * *

When Paul Brown became the coach and general manager of the Cincinnati Bengals and organized the team for their first season in 1968, he asked Phil Samp and me to be the team's play-by-play announcers for the Bengals' Radio Network. At that time, the station was still televising Ohio State basketball games, and my job with the Bengals didn't sit well with the university.

The Ohio State University Athletic Department contacted station management and asked that I be removed from doing Ohio State basketball games on Channel 4, since I was part of the Bengals' play-by-play team on radio. They were so simon pure that they didn't think it was right.

It didn't work. I was not kicked off the broadcast, and for a number of years continued to do both Ohio State basketball on TV and Cincinnati Bengals games on radio.

* * * *

In 1968, Paul Robinson, a running back out of Arizona, was the Bengals' third-round draft pick. He'd played only one year of college football and had been a track star for his last three years. It was a great pick by the Bengals. Robinson gained 1,023 yards rushing and was the AFL and American Football Conference Rookie of the Year.

I particularly remember a game against the Dolphins in Miami, when Robinson showed his running prowess. His first touchdown run was 55 yards. At the line of scrimmage, every defensive lineman was knocked off his feet. The linebackers were knocked out of position, along with the cornerbacks. The only person Paul Robinson had to beat was the free safety. All he had to do was give him a little juke step and—bingo!—head for the goal line.

Paul Brown had always told his running backs and wide receivers to level off and head for the goal line when they had the ball. In this case Paul Robinson had faked the safety out and had a straight shot to the goal line.

He was at the hash mark on the far side of the field. All of a sudden, at about the 30 yard line, we saw him come across the field clear over to the other hash mark, down that hash mark and then, like he was running a post pattern, he ran on to the goal post. So to go 55 yards, he ran about 70 yards.

He came back to the sideline after making the touchdown, and my broadcasting partner and I, Phil Samp, watched as his teammates congratulated him and Paul Brown spoke to him.

That night, as we were flying back to Cincinnati, Paul Brown told us he'd said, "What the hell were you doing all that running over on the other side of the field for?"

Robinson had given him a big smile and replied,"Coach, this game is being televised nationally and my folks are watching. The cameras are over on that other side of the field, and I knew they'd see me a lot better if I ran over there."

After relating the story, Paul Brown said, "I had to turn my back on Robinson or I would have laughed in his face. I couldn't argue with that kind of logic."

* * * *

During our first Easter Seal Telethon in 1978, which went on the air on a Saturday at 11 p.m., an important electrical component on one of our three cameras went on the fritz about 3 p.m. Sunday. With five hours more to go and no replacement part to be found, it looked as though we'd have to make do with only two cameras. Since the last hours of the telethon tend to bring in the most pledges, losing that one camera meant losing some of our effectiveness with viewers.

Somehow, Gene D'Angelo, general manager of WBNS-TV, found out about our predicament. He called the folks at TV-4 and told them he'd send over the spare part we so desperately needed for that camera. Now, that's an example of "Class" with a capital "C!"

* * * *

I'll be forever indebted to the late John Galbreath for his many kindnesses, his thoughtfulness, and his generosity. I met him back in 1963, shortly after I returned from the Pan American Games in Sao Paulo, when we did a one hour documentary on Mr. Galbreath and his Kentucky Derby winner, Chateaugay.

That summer, we spent the better part of four months with Mr. Galbreath, traveling all over the country with him to put together the film clips necessary for the show. We traveled mainly in Kentucky and New York, filming all of the activities associated with Chateaugay.

Many years later, when his Pittsburgh Pirates were playing the San Francisco Giants in the National League playoffs, Mr. Galbreath invited a number of reporters to go to Pittsburgh to see the playoff games. We met at Darby Dan Farm, where his corporate jets spirited us off to the Pittsburgh airport. From there, several of his people picked us up and drove us to Three Rivers Stadium.

The car I walked up to was driven by none other than John Galbreath, who was then in his seventies. He was the most effervescent man I've ever met, and he had two speeds, fast and faster.

On the way to the stadium, he drove 60 to 65 miles an hour—all the while looking around at his passengers and talking about his beloved Pittsburgh Pirates. All of us wondered if we were going to get to that stadium alive! We later joked that it was worth it to ride with the highest-priced driver in the United States, multi-millionaire John Galbreath.

* * * *

In the summer of 1992, I was playing a round of golf at Wedgewood Golf and Country Club with three friends, one of whom was Dr. Doug Shilliday.

Our ninth hole was about five hundred yards from the tees we were playing and we had a heck of wind behind us. I hit a driver—just hit it on the screws—hit a three-wood the second shot, and I was on the green in two. I had a 12-foot putt for an eagle and I got the eagle. I am just an average golfer, and that was the first eagle I've ever had, so I was overjoyed.

I went to Doug's house for dinner that night and he had apparently already told his wife, Norma, what had happened. When I walked in, Norma gave me a big hug and said, "You had an eagle today, didn't you?"

Feeling very proud of myself, I replied, "I sure did."

Norma stepped back and said, "Just think, if you'd had a double eagle, you could have broken a hundred."

I had to laugh. It was probably the ultimate put-down of all time.

* * * *

One of my friends from college days is Dow Finsterwald, the 1958 U.S. PGA champion. Dow is an Athens, Ohio, native and after he won the championship, the Athens Country Club held a "Dow Finsterwald day." To mark the occasion, Dow, Arnold Palmer, former Big Ten champion Howard Baker Saunders, and a young amateur by the name of Jack Nicklaus played an exhibition round of golf. I was there covering the event for a special show on Channel 4.

As I followed Dow and his wife Linda around the course, I couldn't help comparing his incredible golfing skill with my average abilities at the sport. At one point, I said to him, "Dow, every time you hit a shot like that, I want to go home and break up my clubs and make firewood out of them."

His response made me feel a lot better. "Jim," he told me, "just remember one thing. Every shot I hit, whether it's on tour or at an exhibition match like this one, is directly related to the kind of clothes my family wears, the kind of food we eat, and the kind of roof we have over our heads. This is my business. Until golf becomes that serious to you, just play to have fun."

Over the years, Dow's advice has helped me keep my golf game in perspective. I have also applied his "just go out and have fun" philosophy to my work. Maybe that's why what I do for a living has never felt like work to me.

Besides being my profession, sports reporting has been an avocation, a hobby, a ticket to meeting and learning from some of the most interesting people in the world. It has provided an unparalleled opportunity to go out and have fun.

When I began singing on WMAN with Avis LaVerne Forrest fifty-three years ago, I didn't realize that I was beginning what would become not just a career, but a lifelong adventure in radio and TV. I can honestly say that I've enjoyed every minute of the trip, and all the people I've met along the way.